The Footpath Way
An Anthology for Walkers

Hilaire Belloc et al.

The Footpath Way: An Anthology for Walkers

Copyright © 2020 Bibliotech Press
All rights reserved

The present edition is a reproduction of previous publication of this classic work. Minor typographical errors may have been corrected without note, however, for an authentic reading experience the spelling, punctuation, and capitalization have been retained from the original text.

ISBN: 978-1-64799-191-3

ACKNOWLEDGMENTS

The thanks of the publishers are due to: Messrs Chatto & Windus, Messrs Duckworth, and Messrs Houghton Miflin of Boston, U.S.A., for permission to include R. L. Stevenson's *Walking Tours*; Sir Leslie Stephen's *In Praise of Walking*; and Mr John Burroughs' *The Exhilarations of the Road*, from "Winter Sunshine"; also to Mr A. H. Bullen for the extract from *The Gentleman's Magazine*.

CONTENTS

	PAGE
INTRODUCTION	vi
H. Belloc	
WALKING AN ANTIDOTE TO CITY POISON	1
Sidney Smith	
ON GOING A JOURNEY	2
William Hazlitt	
THE BISHOP OF SALISBURY'S HORSE	12
Izaak Walton	
A STROLLING PEDLAR	13
Sir Walter Scott	
A STOUT PEDESTRIAN	15
Sir Walter Scott	
LAKE SCENERY	18
William Wordsworth	
WALKING, AND THE WILD	20
H. D. Thoreau	
A YOUNG TRAMP	46
Charles Dickens	
"BETTER THAN THE GIG!"	48
Charles Dickens	
DE QUINCEY LEADS THE SIMPLE LIFE	50
Thomas de Quincey	
	53

A RESOLUTION

George Borrow

THE SNOWDON RANGER   62

George Borrow

SONG OF THE OPEN ROAD   69

Walt Whitman

WALKING TOURS   79

R. L. Stevenson

SYLVANUS URBAN DISCOVERS A GOOD BREW 86

Gentleman's Magazine

MINCHMOOR   87

Dr John Brown

IN PRAISE OF WALKING   97

Leslie Stephen

THE EXHILARATIONS OF THE ROAD   112

John Burroughs

Introduction

So long as man does not bother about what he is or whence he came or whither he is going, the whole thing seems as simple as the verb "to be"; and you may say that the moment he does begin thinking about what he is (which is more than thinking that he is) and whence he came and whither he is going, he gets on to a lot of roads that lead nowhere, and that spread like the fingers of a hand or the sticks of a fan; so that if he pursues two or more of them he soon gets beyond his straddle, and if he pursues only one he gets farther and farther from the rest of all knowledge as he proceeds. You may say that and it will be true. But there is one kind of knowledge a man does get when he thinks about what he is, whence he came and whither he is going, which is this: that it is the only important question he can ask himself.

Now the moment a man begins asking himself those questions (and all men begin at some time or another if you give them rope enough) man finds himself a very puzzling fellow. There was a school—it can hardly be called a school of philosophy—and it is now as dead as mutton, but anyhow there *was* a school which explained the business in the very simple method known to the learned as tautology—that is, saying the same thing over and over again. For just as the woman in Molière was dumb because she was affected with the quality of dumbness, so man, according to this school, did all the extraordinary things he does do because he had developed in that way. They took in a lot of people while they were alive (I believe a few of the very old ones still survive), they took in nobody more than themselves; but they have not taken in any of the younger generation. We who come after these scientists continue to ask ourselves the old question, and if there is no finding of an answer to it, so much the worse; for asking it, every instinct of our nature tells us, is the proper curiosity of man.

Of the great many things which man does which he should not do or need not do, if he were wholly explained by the verb "to be," you may count walking. Of course if you build up a long series of guesses as to the steps by which he learnt to walk, and call *that* an explanation, there is no more to be said. It is as though I were to ask you why Mr Smith went to Liverpool, and you were to answer by giving me a list of all the stations between Euston and Lime Street, in their exact order. At least that is what it would be like if your guesses were accurate, not only in their statement, but also in their proportion, and also in their order. It is millions to one that your guesses are nothing of the kind. But even granted by a miracle that you have got them all quite right (which is more than the wildest fanatic would grant to the dearest of his geologians) it tells me nothing.

What on earth persuaded the animal to go on like that? Or was it nothing on earth but something in heaven?

Just watch a man walking, if he is a proper man, and see the business of it: how he expresses his pride, or his determination, or his tenacity, or his curiosity, or perhaps his very purpose in his stride! Well, all that business of walking that you are looking at is a piece of extraordinarily skilful trick-acting, such that were the animal not known to do it you would swear he could never be trained to it by any process, however lengthy, or however minute, or however strict. This is what happens when a man walks: first of all he is in stable equilibrium, though the arc of stability is minute. If he stands with his feet well apart, his centre of gravity (which is about half way up him or a little more) may oscillate within an arc of about five degrees on either side of stability and tend to return to rest. But if it oscillates beyond that five degrees or so, the stability of his equilibrium is lost, and down he comes. Men have been known to sleep standing up without a support, especially on military service, which is the most fatiguing thing in the world; but it is extremely rare, and you may say of a man so standing, even with his feet well spread, that he is already doing a fine athletic feat.

But wait a moment: he desires to go, to proceed, to reach a distant point, and instead of going on all fours, where equilibrium would indeed be stable, what does he do? He deliberately lifts one of his supports off the ground, and sends his equilibrium to the devil; at the same time he leans a little forward so as to make himself fall towards the object he desires to attain. You do not know that he does this, but that is because you are a man and your ignorance of it is like the ignorance in which so many really healthy people stand to religion, or the ignorance of a child who thinks his family established for ever in comfort, wealth and security. What you really do, man, when you want to get to that distant place (and let this be a parable of all adventure and of all desire) is to take an enormous risk, the risk of coming down bang and breaking something: you lift one foot off the ground, and, as though that were not enough, you deliberately throw your centre of gravity forward so that you begin to fall.

That is the first act of the comedy.

The second act is that you check your fall by bringing the foot which you had swung into the air down upon the ground again.

That you would say was enough of a bout. Slide the other foot up, take a rest, get your breath again and glory in your feat. But not a bit of it! The moment you have got that loose foot of yours firm on the earth, you use the impetus of your first tumble to begin another one. You get your centre of gravity by the momentum of your going well forward of the foot that has found the ground, you lift the other foot without a care, you let it swing in the fashion of a pendulum, and you check your second fall in the same manner as you checked your first; and even after that second clever little success you do not bring your feet both firmly to the ground to recover yourself before the next venture: you go on with the business, get your centre of gravity forward of the foot that is now on the ground, swinging the other beyond it like a pendulum, stopping your third catastrophe, and so on; and you have come to do all this so that you think it the most natural thing in the world!

Not only do you manage to do it but you can do it in a thousand ways, as a really clever acrobat will astonish his audience not only by walking on the tight-rope but by eating his dinner on it. You can walk quickly or slowly, or look over your shoulder as you walk, or shoot fairly accurately as you walk; you can saunter, you can force your pace, you can turn which way you will. You certainly did not teach yourself to accomplish this marvel, nor did your nurse. There was a spirit within you that taught you and that brought you out; and as it is with walking, so it is with speech, and so at last with humour and with irony, and with affection, and with the sense of colour and of form, and even with honour, and at last with prayer.

By all this you may see that man is very remarkable, and this should make you humble, not proud; for you have been designed in spite of yourself for some astonishing fate, of which these mortal extravagances so accurately seized and so well moulded to your being are but the symbols.

Walking, like talking (which rhymes with it, I am glad to say), being so natural a thing to man, so varied and so unthought about, is necessarily not only among his chief occupations but among his most entertaining subjects of commonplace and of exercise.

Thus to walk without an object is an intense burden, as it is to talk without an object. To walk because it is good for you warps the soul, just as it warps the soul for a man to talk for hire or because he thinks it his duty. On the other hand, walking with an object brings out all that there is in a man, just as talking with an object does. And those who understand the human body, when they confine themselves to what they know and are therefore legitimately interesting, tell us this very interesting thing which experience proves to be true: that walking of every form of exercise is the most general and the most complete, and that while a man may be endangered by riding a horse or by running or swimming, or while a man may easily exaggerate any violent movement, walking will always be to his benefit—that is, of course, so long as he does not warp his soul by the detestable habit of walking for no object but exercise. For it has been so arranged that the moment we begin any minor and terrestrial thing as an object in itself, or with merely the furtherance of some other material thing, we hurt the inward part of us that governs all. But walk for glory or for adventure, or to see new sights, or to pay a bill or to escape the same, and you will very soon find how consonant is walking with your whole being. The chief proof of this (and how many men have tried it, and in how many books does not that truth shine out!) is the way in which a man walking becomes the cousin or the brother of everything round.

If you will look back upon your life and consider what landscapes remain fixed in your memory, some perhaps you will discover to have struck you at the end of long rides or after you have been driven for hours, dragged by an animal or a machine. But much the most of these visions have come to you when you were performing that little miracle with a description of which I began this: and what is more, the visions that you get when you are walking, merge pleasantly into each other. Some are greater, some lesser, and they make a continuous whole. The great moments are led up to and are fittingly framed.

There is no time or weather, in England at least, in which a man walking does not feel this cousinship with everything round. There are weathers that are intolerable if you are doing anything else but walking: if you are crouching still against a storm or if you are driving against it; or if you are riding in extreme cold; or if you are running too quickly in extreme heat; but it is not so with walking. You may walk by night or by day, in summer or in winter, in fair weather or in foul, in calm or in a gale, and in every case you are doing something native to yourself and going the best way you could go. All men have felt this.

Walking, also from this same natural quality which it has, introduces particular sights to you in their right proportion. A man gets into his motor car, or more likely into somebody else's, and covers a great many miles in a very few hours. And what remains to him at the end of it, when he looks closely into the pictures of his mind, is a curious and unsatisfactory thing: there are patches of blurred nothingness like an uneasy sleep, one or two intense pieces of impression, disconnected, violently vivid and mad, a red cloak, a shining streak of water, and more particularly a point of danger. In all that ribbon of sights, each either much too lightly or much too heavily impressed, he is lucky if there is one great view which for one moment he seized and retained from a height as he whirled along. The whole record is like a bit of dry point that has been done by a hand not sure of itself upon a plate that trembled, now jagged chiselling bit into the metal; now blurred or hardly impressed it at all: only in some rare moment of self-possession or of comparative repose did the hand do what it willed and transfer its power.

You may say that riding upon a horse one has a better chance. That is true, but after all one is busy riding. Look back upon the very many times that you have ridden, and though you will remember many things you will not remember them in that calm and perfect order in which they presented themselves to you when you were afoot. As for a man running, if it be for any distance the effort is so unnatural as to concentrate upon himself all a man's powers, and he is almost blind to exterior things. Men at the end of such efforts are actually and physically blind; they fall helpless.

Then there is the way of looking at the world which rich men imagine they can purchase with money when they build a great house looking over some view—but it is not in the same street with walking! You see the sight nine times out of ten when you are ill attuned to it, when your blood is slow and unmoved, and when the machine is not going. When you are walking the machine is always going, and every sense in you is doing what it should with the right emphasis and in due discipline to make a perfect record of all that is about.

Consider how a man walking approaches a little town; he sees it a long way off upon a hill; he sees its unity, he has time to think about it a great deal. Next it is hidden from him by a wood, or it is screened by a roll of land. He tops this and sees the little town again, now much nearer, and he thinks more particularly of its houses, of the way in which they stand, and of what has passed in them. The sky, especially if it has large white clouds in it and is for the rest sunlit and blue, makes something against which he can see the little town, and gives it life. Then he is at the outskirts, and he does not suddenly occupy it with a clamour or a rush, nor does he merely contemplate it, like a man from a window, unmoving. He enters in. He passes, healthily wearied, human doors and signs; he can note all the names of the people and the trade at which they work; he has time to see their faces. The square broadens before him, or the market-place, and so very naturally and rightly he comes to his inn, and he has fulfilled one of the great ends of man.

Lord, how tempted one is here to make a list of those monsters who are the enemies of inns!

There is your monster who thinks of it as a place to which a man does not walk but into which he slinks to drink; and there is your monster who thinks of it as a place to be reached in a railway train and there to put on fine clothes for dinner and to be waited upon by Germans. There is your more amiable monster, who says: "I hear there is a good inn at Little Studley or Bampton Major. Let us go there." He waits until he has begun to be hungry, and he shoots there in an enormous automobile. There is your still more amiable monster, who in a hippo-mobile hippogriffically tools into a town and throws the ribbons to the person in gaiters with a straw in his mouth, and feels (oh, men, my brothers) that he is doing something like someone in a book. All these men, whether they frankly hate or whether they pretend to love, are the enemies of inns, and the enemies of inns are accursed before their Creator and their kind.

There are some things which are a consolation for Eden and which clearly prove to the heavily-burdened race of Adam that it has retained a memory of diviner things. We have all of us done evil. We have permitted the modern cities to grow up, and we have told such lies that now we are accursed with newspapers. And we have so loved wealth that we are all in debt, and that the poor are a burden to us and the rich are an offence. But we ought to keep up our hearts and not to despair, because we can still all of us pray when there is an absolute necessity to do so, and we have wormed out the way of building up that splendid thing which all over Christendom men know under many names and which is called in England an INN.

I have sometimes wondered when I sat in one of these places, remaking my soul, whether the inn would perish out of Europe. I am convinced the terror was but the terror which we always feel for whatever is exceedingly beloved.

There is an inn in the town of Piacenza into which I once walked while I was still full of immortality, and there I found such good companions and so much marble, rooms so large and empty and so old, and cooking so excellent, that I made certain it would survive even that immortality which, I say, was all around. But no! I came there eight years later, having by that time heard the noise of the Subterranean River and being well conscious of mortality. I came to it as to a friend, and the beastly thing had changed! In place of the grand stone doors there was a sort of twirlygig like the things that let you in to the Zoo, where you pay a shilling, and inside there were decorations made up of meaningless curves like those with which the demons have punished the city of Berlin; the salt at the table was artificial and largely made of chalk, and the faces of the host and hostess were no longer kind.

I very well remember another inn which was native to the Chiltern Hills. This place had bow windows, which were divided into medium-sized panes, each of the panes a little rounded; and these window-panes were made of that sort of glass which I will adore until I die, and which has the property of distorting exterior objects: of such glass the windows of schoolrooms and of nurseries used to be made. I came to that place after many years by accident, and I found that Orcus, which has devoured all lovely things, had devoured this too. The inn was called "an Hotel," its front was rebuilt, the window's had only two panes, each quite enormous and flat, one above and one below, and the glass was that sort of thick, transparent glass through which it is no use to look, for you might as well be looking through air. All the faces were strange except that of one old servant in the stable-yard. I asked him if he regretted the old front, and he said "Lord, no!" Then he told me in great detail how kind the brewers had been to his master and how willingly they had rebuilt the whole place. These things reconcile one with the grave.

Well then, if walking, which has led me into this digression, prepares one for the inns where they are worthy, it has another character as great and as symbolic and as worthy of man. For remember that of the many ways of walking there is one way which is the greatest of all, and that is to walk away.

Put your hand before your eyes and remember, you that have walked, the places from which you have walked away, and the wilderness into which you manfully turned the steps of your abandonment.

There is a place above the Roman Wall beyond the River Tyne where one can do this thing. Behind one lies the hospitality and the human noise which have inhabited the town of the river valley for certainly two thousand years. Before one is the dead line of the road, and that complete emptiness of the moors as they rise up toward Cheviot on the one hand and Carter Fell upon the other. The earth is here altogether deserted and alone: you go out into it because it is your business to go: you are walking away. As for your memories, they are of no good to you except to lend you that dignity which can always support a memoried man; you are bound to forget, and it is your business to leave all that you have known altogether behind you, and no man has eyes at the back of his head—go forward. Upon my soul I think that the greatest way of walking, now I consider the matter, or now that I have stumbled upon it, is walking away.

H. BELLOC.

Walking an Antidote to City Poison

There is moral as well as bodily wholesomeness in a mountain walk, if the walker has the understanding heart, and eschews *picnics*. It is good for any man to be alone with nature and himself, or with a friend who knows when silence is more sociable than talk:

> "In the wilderness alone,
> There where nature worships God."

It is well to be in places where man is little and God is great—where what he sees all around him has the same look as it had a thousand years ago, and will have the same, in all likelihood, when he has been a thousand years in his grave. It abates and rectifies a man, if he is worth the process.

It is not favourable to religious feeling to hear only of the actions and interference of man, and to behold nothing but what human ingenuity has completed. There is an image of God's greatness impressed upon the outward face of nature fitted to make us all pious, and to breathe into our hearts a purifying and salutary fear.

In cities everything is man, and man alone. He seems to move and govern all, and be the Providence of cities; and there we do not render unto Cæsar the things which are Cæsar's, and unto God the things which are God's; but God is forgotten, and Cæsar is supreme—all is human policy, human foresight, human power; nothing reminds us of *invisible dominion, and concealed omnipotence*—it is all earth, and no heaven. One cure of this is prayer and the solitary place. As the body, harassed with the noxious air of cities, seeks relief in the freedom and the purity of the fields and hills, so the mind, wearied by commerce with men, resumes its vigour in solitude, and repairs its dignity.

Sydney Smith.

On Going a Journey

One of the pleasantest things in the world is going a journey; but I like to go by myself. I can enjoy society in a room; but out of doors nature is company enough for me. I am then never less alone than when alone.

"The fields his study, nature was his book."

I cannot see the wit of walking and talking at the same time. When I am in the country, I wish to vegetate like the country. I am not for criticising hedgerows and black cattle. I go out of the town in order to forget the town and all that is in it. There are those who for this purpose go to watering-places, and carry the metropolis with them. I like more elbow-room, and fewer encumbrances. I like solitude, when I give myself up to it, for the sake of solitude; nor do I ask for

"A friend in my retreat,
Whom I may whisper solitude is sweet."

The soul of a journey is liberty, perfect liberty, to think, feel, do, just as one pleases. We go a journey chiefly to be free of all impediments and of all inconveniences; to leave ourselves behind, much more to get rid of others. It is because I want a little breathing-space to muse on indifferent matters, where Contemplation

"May plume her feathers, and let grow her wings
That in the various bustle of resort
Were all too ruffled, and sometimes impair'd,"

that I absent myself from the town for a while without feeling at a loss the moment I am left by myself. Instead of a friend in a post-chaise or in a Tilbury, to exchange good things with and vary the same stale topics over again, for once let me have a truce with impertinence. Give me the clear blue sky over my head and the green turf beneath my feet, a winding road before me, and a three hours' march to dinner—and then to thinking! It is hard if I cannot start some game on these lone heaths. I laugh, I run, I leap, I sing for joy. From the point of yonder rolling cloud, I plunge into my past being, and revel there, as the sunburnt Indian plunges headlong into the wave that wafts him to his native shore. Then long-forgotten things, like "sunken wrack and sumless treasuries," burst upon my eager sight, and I begin to feel, think, and be myself again. Instead of an awkward silence, broken by attempts at wit or dull commonplaces, mine is that undisturbed silence of the heart which alone is perfect eloquence.

No one likes puns, alliterations, antitheses, argument, and analysis better than I do; but I sometimes had rather be without them. "Leave, oh, leave me to my repose!" I have just now other business in hand, which would seem idle to you; but is with me "very stuff o' the conscience." Is not this wild rose sweet without a comment? Does not this daisy leap to my heart set in its coat of emerald? Yet if I were to explain to you the circumstance that has so endeared it to me, you would only smile. Had I not better, then, keep it to myself, and let it serve me to brood over, from here to yonder craggy point, and from thence onward to the far-distant horizon? I should be but bad company all that way, and therefore prefer being alone.

I have heard it said that you may, when the moody fit comes on, walk or ride on by yourself, and indulge your reveries. But this looks like a breach of manners, a neglect of others, and you are thinking all the time that you ought to rejoin your party. "Out upon such half-faced fellowship!" say I. I like to be either entirely to myself, or entirely at the disposal of others; to talk or be silent, to walk or sit still, to be sociable or solitary. I was pleased with an observation of Mr Cobbett's, that "he thought it a bad French custom to drink our wine with our meals, and that an Englishman ought to do only one thing at a time." So I cannot talk and think, or indulge in melancholy musing and lively conversation, by fits and starts. "Let me have a companion of my way," says Sterne, "were it but to remark how the shadows lengthen as the sun declines." It is beautifully said; but, in my opinion, this continual comparing of notes interferes with the involuntary impression of things upon the mind, and hurts the sentiment.

If you only hint what you feel in a kind of dumb show, it is insipid; if you have to explain it, it is making a toil of a pleasure. You cannot read the book of nature without being perpetually put to the trouble of translating it for the benefit of others. I am for this synthetical method on a journey in preference to the analytical. I am content to lay in a stock of ideas then, and to examine and anatomise them afterwards. I want to see my vague notions float like the down of the thistle before the breeze, and not to have them entangled in the briars and thorns of controversy. For once, I like to have it all my own way; and this is impossible unless you are alone, or in such company as I do not covet. I have no objection to argue a point with anyone for twenty miles of measured road, but not for pleasure. If you remark the scent of a beanfield crossing the road, perhaps your fellow-traveller has no smell. If you point to a distant object, perhaps he is short-sighted, and has to take out his glass to look at it. There is a feeling in the air, a tone in the colour of a cloud, which hits your fancy, but the effect of which you are unable to account for. There is then no sympathy, but an uneasy craving after it, and a dissatisfaction which pursues you on the way, and in the end probably produces ill-humour.

Now, I never quarrel with myself, and take all my own conclusions for granted till I find it necessary to defend them against objections. It is not merely that you may not be of accord on the objects and circumstances that present themselves before you—these may recall a number of objects, and lead to associations too delicate and refined to be possibly communicated to others. Yet these I love to cherish, and sometimes still fondly clutch them, when I can escape from the throng to do so. To give way to our feelings before company seems extravagance or affectation; and, on the other hand, to have to unravel this mystery of our being at every turn, and to make others take an equal interest in it (otherwise the end is not answered), is a task to which few are competent. We must "give it an understanding, but no tongue." My old friend Coleridge, however, could do both. He could go on in the most delightful explanatory way over hill and dale a summer's day, and convert a landscape into a didactic poem or a Pindaric ode. "He talked far above singing." If I could so clothe my ideas in sounding and flowing words, I might perhaps wish to have some one with me to admire the swelling theme; or I could be more content, were it possible for me still to hear his echoing voice in the woods of All-Foxden. They had "that fine madness in them which our first poets had"; and if they could have been caught by some rare instrument, would have breathed such strains as the following:—

"Here be woods as green
  As any, air likewise as fresh and sweet
  As when smooth Zephyrus plays on the fleet
Face of the curled stream, with flow'rs as many
As the young spring gives, and as choice as any;
Here be all new delights, cool streams and wells,
Arbours o'ergrown with woodbines, caves and dells;

> Choose where thou wilt, whilst I sit by and sing,
> Or gather rushes to make many a ring
> For thy long fingers; tell thee tales of love,
> How the pale Phœbe, hunting in a grove,
> First saw the boy Endymion, from whose eyes
> She took eternal fire that never dies;
> How she conveyed him softly in a sleep,
> His temples bound with poppy, to the steep
> Head of old Latmos, where she stoops each night,
> Gilding the mountain with her brother's light,
> To kiss her sweetest."
>
> (FLETCHER'S "Faithful Shepherdess.")

Had I words and images at command like these, I would attempt to wake the thoughts that lie slumbering on golden ridges in the evening clouds; but at the sight of nature my fancy, poor as it is, droops and closes up its leaves, like flowers at sunset. I can make nothing out on the spot: I must have time to collect myself.

In general, a good thing spoils out-of-door prospects; it should be reserved for Table-Talk. Lamb is, for this reason, I take it, the worst company in the world out of doors; because he is the best within. I grant there is one subject on which it is pleasant to talk on a journey, and that is, what we shall have for supper when we get to our inn at night. The open air improves this sort of conversation or friendly altercation, by setting a keener edge on appetite. Every mile of the road heightens the flavour of the viands we expect at the end of it. How fine it is to enter some old town, walled and turreted, just at the approach of nightfall; or to come to some straggling village, with the lights streaming through the surrounding gloom; and then after inquiring for the best entertainment that the place affords, to "take one's ease at one's inn!"

These eventful moments in our lives' history are too precious, too full of solid, heartfelt happiness, to be frittered and dribbled away in imperfect sympathy. I would have them all to myself, and drain them to the last drop; they will do to talk of or to write about afterwards. What a delicate speculation it is, after drinking whole goblets of tea,

> "The cups that cheer, but not inebriate,"

and letting the fumes ascend into the brain, to sit considering what we shall have for supper—eggs and a rasher, a rabbit smothered in onions, or an excellent veal-cutlet! Sancho in such a situation once fixed on cow-heel; and his choice, though he could not help it, is not to be disparaged. Then, in the intervals of pictured scenery and Shandean contemplation, to catch the preparation and the stir in the kitchen (getting ready for the gentleman in the parlour). *Procul, o procul este profani!* These hours are sacred to silence and to musing, to be treasured up in the memory, and to feed the source of smiling thoughts hereafter. I would not waste them in idle talk; or if I must have the integrity of fancy broken in upon, I would rather it were by a stranger than a friend.

A stranger takes his hue and character from the time and place; he is a part of the furniture and costume of an inn. If he is a Quaker, or from the West Riding of Yorkshire, so much the better. I do not even try to sympathise with him, and he breaks no squares. How I love to see the camps of the gypsies, and to sigh my soul into that sort of life! If I express this feeling to another, he may qualify and spoil it with some objection. I associate nothing with my travelling companion but present objects and passing events. In his ignorance of me and my affairs, I in a manner forget myself. But a friend reminds me of other things, rips up old grievances, and destroys the abstraction of the scene. He comes in ungraciously between us and our imaginary character. Something is dropped in the course of conversation that gives a hint of your profession and pursuits; or from having some one with you that knows the less sublime portions of your history, it seems that other people do. You are no longer a citizen of the world; but your "unhoused free condition is put into circumspection and confine."

The *incognito* of an inn is one of its striking privileges—"lord of one's self, uncumbered with a name." Oh, it is great to shake off the trammels of the world and of public opinion; to lose our importunate, tormenting, everlasting personal identity in the elements of nature, and become the creature of the moment, clear of all ties; to hold to the universe only by a dish of sweetbreads, and to owe nothing but the score of the evening; and no longer seeking for applause and meeting with contempt, to be known by no other title than *the gentleman in the parlour*!

One may take one's choice of all characters in this romantic state of uncertainty as to one's real pretensions, and become indefinitely respectable and negatively right-worshipful. We baffle prejudice and disappoint conjecture; and from being so to others, begin to be objects of curiosity and wonder even to ourselves. We are no more those hackneyed commonplaces that we appear in the world; an inn restores us to the level of nature, and quits scores with society! I have certainly spent some enviable hours at inns—sometimes when I have been left entirely to myself, and have tried to solve some metaphysical problem, as once at Witham Common, where I found out the proof that likeness is not a case of the association of ideas— at other times, when there have been pictures in the room, as at St Neot's (I think it was), where I first met with Gribelins' engravings of the Cartoons, into which I entered at once, and at a little inn on the borders of Wales, where there happened to be hanging some of Westall's drawings, which I compared triumphantly (for a theory that I had, not for the admired artist) with the figure of a girl who had ferried me over the Severn standing up in a boat between me and the twilight. At other times I might mention luxuriating in books, with a peculiar interest in this way, as I remember sitting up half the night to read *Paul and Virginia*, which I picked up at an inn at Bridgewater, after being drenched in the rain all day; and at the same place I got through two volumes of Madame D'Arblay's *Camilla*.

It was on the 10th of April 1798, that I sat down to a volume of the *New Heloïse*, at the inn at Llangollen, over a bottle of sherry and a cold chicken. The letter I chose was that in which St Preux describes his feelings as he first caught a glimpse from the heights of the Jura of the Pays de Vaud, which I had brought with me as a *bon bouche* to crown the evening with. It was my birthday, and I had for the first time come from a place in the neighbourhood to visit this delightful spot. The road to Llangollen turns off between Chirk and Wrexham; and on passing a certain point you come all at once upon the valley, which opens like an amphitheatre, broad, barren hills rising in majestic state on either side, with "green upland swells that echo to the bleat of flocks" below, and the river Dee babbling over its stony bed in the midst of them. The valley at this time "glittered green with sunny showers," and a budding ash-tree dipped its tender branches in the chiding stream.

How proud, how glad I was to walk along the highroad that overlooks the delicious prospect, repeating the lines which I have just quoted from Mr Coleridge's poems! But besides the prospect which opened beneath my feet, another also opened to my inward sight, a heavenly vision on which were written in letters large as Hope could make them, these fourwords, LIBERTY, GENIUS, LOVE,

VIRTUE, which have since faded into the light of the common day, or mock my idle gaze.

"The beautiful is vanished, and returns not."

Still, I would return some time or other to this enchanted spot; but I would return to it alone. What other self could I find to share that influx of thoughts, of regret, and delight, the fragments of which I could hardly conjure up to myself, so much have they been broken and defaced? I could stand on some tall rock, and overlook the precipice of years that separates me from what I then was. I was at that time going shortly to visit the poet whom I have above named. Where is he now? Not only I myself have changed; the world, which was then new to me, has become old and incorrigible. Yet will I turn to thee in thought, O sylvan Dee, in joy, in youth and gladness, as thou then wert; and thou shalt always be to me the river of Paradise, where I will drink of the waters of life freely!

There is hardly anything that shows the short-sightedness or capriciousness of the imagination more than travelling does. With change of place we change our ideas; nay, our opinions and feelings. We can by an effort, indeed, transport ourselves to old and long-forgotten scenes, and then the picture of the mind revives again; but we forget those that we have just left. It seems that we can think but of one place at a time. The canvas of the fancy is but of a certain extent, and if we paint one set of objects upon it, they immediately efface every other. We cannot enlarge our conceptions, we only shift our point of view. The landscape bares its bosom to the enraptured eye; we take our fill of it, and seem as if we could form no other image of beauty or grandeur. We pass on, and think no more of it: the horizon that shuts it from our sight also blots it from our memory like a dream. In travelling through a wild, barren country, I can form no idea of a woody and cultivated one. It appears to me that all the world must be barren, like what I see of it. In the country we forget the town, and in town we despise the country. "Beyond Hyde Park," says Sir Fopling Flutter, "all is a desert." All that part of the map that we do not see before us is blank. The world in our conceit of it is not much bigger than a nutshell. It is not one prospect expanded into another, county joined to county, kingdom to kingdom, land to seas, making an image voluminous and vast; the mind can form no larger idea of space than the eye can take in at a single glance. The rest is a name written in a map, a calculation of arithmetic.

For instance, what is the true signification of that immense mass of territory and population known by the name of China to us? An inch of pasteboard on a wooden globe, of no more account than a china orange! Things near us are seen of the size of life; things at a distance are diminished to the size of the understanding. We measure the universe by ourselves, and even comprehend the texture of our own being only piecemeal. In this way, however, we remember an infinity of things and places. The mind is like a mechanical instrument that plays a great variety of tunes, but it must play them in succession. One idea recalls another, but at the same time excludes all others. In trying to renew old recollections, we cannot as it were unfold the whole web of our existence; we must pick out the single threads. So in coming to a place where we have formerly lived, and with which we have intimate associations, every one must have found that the feeling grows more vivid the nearer we approach the spot, from the mere anticipation of the actual impression: we remember circumstances, feelings, persons, faces, names that we had not thought of for years; but for the time all the rest of the world is forgotten! To return to the question I have quitted above:

I have no objection to go to see ruins, aqueducts, pictures, in company with a friend or a party, but rather the contrary, for the former reason reversed. They are intelligible matters, and will bear talking about. The sentiment here is not tacit, but communicable and overt. Salisbury Plain is barren of criticism, but Stonehenge will bear a discussion antiquarian, picturesque, and philosophical. In setting out on a party of pleasure, the first consideration always is where we shall go to: in taking a solitary ramble, the question is what we shall meet with by the way. "The mind is its own place"; nor are we anxious to arrive at the end of our journey. I can myself do the honours indifferently well to the works of art and curiosity. I once took a party to Oxford, with no mean *éclat*—showed them that seat of the Muses at a distance,

"With glistering spires and pinnacles adorn'd,"

descanted on the learned air that breathes from the grassy quadrangles and stone walls of halls and colleges; was at home in the Bodleian; and at Blenheim quite superseded the powdered cicerone that attended us, and that pointed in vain with his wand to commonplace beauties in matchless pictures.

As another exception to the above reasoning, I should not feel confident in venturing on a journey in a foreign country without a companion. I should want at intervals to hear the sound of my own language. There is an involuntary antipathy in the mind of an Englishman to foreign manners and notions that requires the assistance of social sympathy to carry it off. As the distance from home increases, this relief, which was at first a luxury, becomes a passion and an appetite. A person would almost feel stifled to find himself in the deserts of Arabia without friends and countrymen: there must be allowed to be something in the view of Athens or old Rome that claims the utterance of speech; and I own that the Pyramids are too mighty for any single contemplation. In such situations, so opposite to all one's ordinary train of ideas, one seems a species by one's self, a limb torn off from society, unless one can meet with instant fellowship and support.

Yet I did not feel this want or craving very pressing once, when I first set my foot on the laughing shores of France. Calais was peopled with novelty and delight. The confused, busy murmur of the place was like oil and wine poured into my ears; nor did the mariners' hymn, which was sung from the top of an old crazy vessel in the harbour, as the sun went down, send an alien sound into my soul. I only breathed the air of general humanity. I walked over "the vine-covered hills and gay regions of France," erect and satisfied; for the image of man was not cast down and chained to the foot of arbitrary thrones: I was at no loss for language, for that of all the great schools of painting was open to me. The whole is vanished like a shade. Pictures, heroes, glory, freedom, all are fled; nothing remains but the Bourbons and the French people!

There is undoubtedly a sensation in travelling into foreign parts that is to be had nowhere else; but it is more pleasing at the time than lasting. It is too remote from our habitual associations to be a common topic of discourse or reference, and, like a dream or another state of existence, does not piece into our daily modes of life. It is an animated but a momentary hallucination. It demands an effort to exchange our actual for our ideal identity; and to feel the pulse of our old transports revive very keenly, we must "jump" all our present comforts and connections. Our romantic and itinerant character is not to be domesticated. Dr Johnson remarked how little foreign travel added to the facilities of conversation in those who had been abroad. In fact, the time we have spent there is both delightful and, in one sense, instructive; but it appears to be cut out of our substantial downright existence, and never to join kindly on to it. We are not the same, but another, and perhaps more enviable individual all the time we are out of our own country. We are lost to ourselves as well as to our friends. So the poet somewhat quaintly sings:

"Out of my country and myself I go."

Those who wish to forget painful thoughts do well to absent themselves for a while from the ties and objects that recall them: but we can be said only to fulfil our destiny in the place that gave us birth. I should on this account like well enough to spend the whole of my life in travelling abroad, if I could anywhere borrow another life to spend afterwards at home!

William Hazlitt.

The Bishop of Salisbury's Horse

As soon as he was perfectly recovered of this sickness, he took a journey from Oxford to Exeter, to satisfy and see his good Mother, being accompanied with a countryman and companion of his own College, and both on foot; which was then either more in fashion, or want of money, or their humility made it so: but on foot they went, and took Salisbury on their way, purposely to see the good Bishop, who made Mr Hooker and his companion dine with him at his own table: which Mr Hooker boasted of with much joy and gratitude when he saw his mother and friends: and at the Bishop's parting with him, the Bishop gave him good counsel, and his benediction, but forgot to give him money; which when the Bishop had considered, he sent a servant in all haste to call Richard back to him: and at Richard's return, the Bishop said to him, "Richard, I sent for you back to lend you a horse, which hath carried me many a mile, and, I thank God, with much ease"; and presently delivered into his hand a walking-staff, with which he professed he had travelled through many parts of Germany. And he said, "Richard, I do not give, but lend you my horse: be sure you be honest, and bring my horse back to me at your return this way to Oxford. And I do now give you ten groats, to bear your charges to Exeter: and here is ten groats more, which I charge you to deliver to your Mother and tell her I send her a Bishop's benediction with it, and beg the continuance of her prayers for me. And if you bring my horse back to me, I will give you ten groats more, to carry you on foot to the College, and so God bless you, good Richard."

Izaak Walton.

A Strolling Pedlar

My frame gradually became hardened with my constitution, and being both tall and muscular, I was rather disfigured than disabled by my lameness. This personal disadvantage did not prevent me from taking much exercise on horseback, and making long journeys on foot, in the course of which I often walked from twenty to thirty miles a day.

A distinct instance occurs to me. I remember walking with poor James Ramsay, my fellow-apprentice, now no more, and two other friends, to breakfast at Prestonpans. We spent the forenoon visiting the ruins at Seton and the field of battle at Preston—dined at Prestonpans on tiled haddocks very sumptuously—drank half a bottle of port each, and returned in the evening. This could not be less than thirty miles, nor do I remember being at all fatigued upon the occasion.

These excursions on foot and horseback formed by far my most favourite amusement. I have all my life delighted in travelling, though I have never enjoyed that pleasure upon a large scale. It was a propensity which I sometimes indulged so unduly as to alarm and vex my parents. Wood, water, wilderness itself had an inexpressible charm for me, and I had a dreamy way of going much farther than I intended, so that unconsciously my return was protracted, and my parents had sometimes serious cause of uneasiness. For example, I once set out with Mr George Abercromby (son of the immortal general), Mr William Clerk, and some others, to fish in the lake above Howgate, and the stream which descends from it into the Esk. We breakfasted at Howgate, and fished the whole day; and while we were on our return next morning, I was easily seduced by William Clerk, then a great intimate, to visit Pennycuik House, the seat of his family. Here he and John Irving, and I for their sake, were overwhelmed with kindness by the late Sir John Clerk and his lady, the present Dowager Lady Clerk. The pleasure of looking at fine pictures, the beauty of the place, and the flattering hospitality of the owners, drowned all recollection of home for a day or two. Meanwhile our companions, who had walked on without being aware of our digression, returned to Edinburgh without us, and excited no small alarm in my father's household. At length, however, they became accustomed to my escapades. My father used to protest to me on such occasions that he thought I was born to be a strolling pedlar; and though the prediction was intended to mortify my conceit, I am not sure that I altogether disliked it. I was now familiar with Shakespeare, and thought of Autolycus's song:

> "Jog on, jog on the footpath way
> And merrily hent the stile-a;
> A merry heart goes all the day,
> Your sad tires in a mile-a."
>
> Sir Walter Scott.

A Stout Pedestrian

Let the reader conceive to himself a clear frosty November morning, the scene an open heath, having for the background that huge chain of mountains in which Skiddaw and Saddleback are preeminent; let him look along that *blind road*, by which I mean the track so slightly marked by the passengers' footsteps that it can but be traced by a slight shade of verdure from the darker heath around it, and, being only visible to the eye when at some distance, ceases to be distinguished while the foot is actually treading it—along this faintly-traced path advances the object of our present narrative. His firm step, his erect and free carriage, have a military air, which corresponds well with his well-proportioned limbs, and stature of six feet high. His dress is so plain and simple that it indicates nothing as to rank—it may be that of a gentleman who travels in this manner for his pleasure, or of an inferior person of whom it is the proper and usual garb. Nothing can be on a more reduced scale than his travelling equipment. A volume of Shakespeare in each pocket, a small bundle with a change of linen slung across his shoulders, an oaken cudgel in his hand, complete our pedestrian's accommodations, and in this equipage we present him to our readers.

Brown had parted that morning from his friend Dudley, and began his solitary walk towards Scotland.

The first two or three miles were rather melancholy, from want of the society to which he had of late been accustomed. But this unusual mood of mind soon gave way to the influence of his natural good spirits, excited by the exercise and the bracing effects of the frosty air. He whistled as he went along, not "from want of thought," but to give vent to those buoyant feelings which he had no other mode of expressing. For each peasant whom he chanced to meet, he had a kind greeting or a good-humoured jest; the hardy Cumbrians grinned as they passed, and said, "That's a kind heart, God bless un!" and the market-girl looked more than once over her shoulder at the athletic form, which corresponded so well with the frank and blithe address of the stranger. A rough terrier dog, his constant companion, who rivalled his master in glee, scampered at large in a thousand wheels round the heath, and came back to jump up on him, and assure him that he participated in the pleasure of the journey. Dr Johnson thought life had few things better than the excitation produced by being whirled rapidly along in a post-chaise; but he who has in youth experienced the confident and independent feeling of a stout pedestrian in an interesting country, and during fine weather, will hold the taste of the great moralist cheap in comparison.

Part of Brown's view in choosing that unusual tract which leads through the eastern walls of Cumberland into Scotland, had been a desire to view the remains of the celebrated Roman Wall, which are more visible in that direction than in any other part of its extent. His education had been imperfect and desultory; but neither the busy scenes in which he had been engaged, nor the pleasures of youth, nor the precarious state of his own circumstances, had diverted him from the task of mental improvement.—"And this then is the Roman Wall," he said, scrambling up to a height which commanded the course of that celebrated work of antiquity: "What a people! whose labours, even at this extremity of their empire, comprehended such space, and were executed upon a scale of such grandeur! In future ages, when the science of war shall have changed, how few traces will exist of the labours of Vauban and Coehorn, while this wonderful people's remains will even then continue to interest and astonish posterity! Their fortifications, their aqueducts, their theatres, their fountains, all their public works, bear the grave, solid, and majestic character of their language; while our modern labours, like our modern tongues, seem but constructed out of their fragments." Having thus moralised, he remembered that he was hungry, and pursued his walk to a small public-house at which he proposed to get some refreshment.

The alehouse, for it was no better, was situated in the bottom of a little dell, through which trilled a small rivulet. It was shaded by a large ash-tree, against which the clay-built shed, that served the purpose of a stable, was erected, and upon which it seemed partly to recline. In this shed stood a saddled horse, employed in eating his corn. The cottages in this part of Cumberland partake of the rudeness which characterises those of Scotland. The outside of the house promised little for the interior, notwithstanding the vaunt of a sign, where a tankard of ale voluntarily decanted itself into a tumbler, and a hieroglyphical scrawl below attempted to express a promise of "good entertainment for man and horse." Brown was no fastidious traveller—he stooped and entered the cabaret.

The first object which caught his eye in the kitchen was a tall, stout, country-looking man, in a large jockey great-coat, the owner of the horse which stood in the shed, who was busy discussing huge slices of cold boiled beef, and casting from time to time an eye through the window, to see how his steed sped with his provender. A large tankard of ale flanked his plate of victuals, to which he applied himself by intervals. The good woman of the house was employed in baking. The fire, as is usual in that country, was on a stone hearth, in the midst of an immensely large chimney, which had two seats extended beneath the vent. On one of these sat a remarkably tall woman, in a red cloak and slouched bonnet, having the appearance of a tinker or beggar. She was busily engaged with a short black tobacco-pipe.

At the request of Brown for some food, the landlady wiped with her mealy apron one corner of the deal table, placed a wooden trencher and knife and fork before the traveller, pointed to the round of beef, recommended Mr Dinmont's good example, and, finally, filled a brown pitcher with her home-brewed. Brown lost no time in doing ample credit to both. For a while, his opposite neighbour and he were too busy to take much notice of each other, except by a good-humoured nod as each in turn raised the tankard to his head. At length, when our pedestrian began to supply the wants of little Wasp, the Scotch store-farmer, for such was Mr Dinmont, found himself at leisure to enter into conversation.

Sir Walter Scott,—"Guy Mannering."

Lake Scenery

The morning was clear and cheerful after a night of sharp frost. At ten o'clock we took our way on foot towards Pooley Bridge on the same side of the lake we had coasted in a boat the day before.—Looked backwards to the south from our favourite station above Blowick. The dazzling sunbeams striking upon the church and village, while the earth was steaming with exhalations not traceable in other quarters, rendered their forms even more indistinct than the partial and flitting veil of unillumined vapour had done two days before. The grass on which we trod, and the trees in every thicket, were dripping with melted hoar-frost. We observed the lemon-coloured leaves of the birches, as the breeze turned them to the sun, sparkle, or rather *flash*, like diamonds, and the leafless purple twigs were tipped with globes of shining crystal.

The day continued delightful, and unclouded to the end. I will not describe the country which we slowly travelled through nor relate our adventures; and will only add, that on the afternoon of the thirteenth we returned along the banks of Ulswater by the usual road. The lake lay in deep repose after the agitations of a wet and stormy morning. The trees in Gowbarrow park were in that state when what is gained by the exposure of their bark and branches compensates, almost, for the loss of foliage, exhibiting the variety which characterises the point of time between autumn and winter. The hawthorns were leafless; their round heads covered with rich scarlet berries, and adorned with arches of green brambles, and eglantines hung with glossy hips; and the grey trunks of some of the ancient oak, which in the summer season might have been regarded only for their venerable majesty, now attracted notice by a pretty embellishment of green mosses and fern intermixed with russet leaves retained by those slender outstarting twigs which the veteran tree would not have tolerated in his strength.

The smooth silver branches of the ashes were bare; most of the alders as green as the Devonshire cottage-myrtle that weathers the snows of Christmas.—Will you accept it as some apology for my having dwelt so long on the woodland ornaments of these scenes—that artists speak of the trees on the banks of Ulswater, and especially along the bays of Stybarrow crags, as having a peculiar character of picturesque intricacy in their stems and branches, which their rocky stations and the mountain winds have combined to give them?

At the end of Gowbarrow park a large herd of deer were either moving slowly or standing still among the fern.

I was sorry when a chance-companion, who had joined us by the way, startled them with a whistle, disturbing an image of grave simplicity and thoughtful enjoyment; for I could have fancied that those natives of this wild and beautiful region were partaking with us a sensation of the solemnity of the closing day. The sun had been set some time; and we could perceive that the light was fading away from the coves of Helvellyn, but the lake under a luminous sky, was more brilliant than before. After tea at Patterdale, set out again:—a fine evening; the seven stars close to the mountain-top; all the stars seemed brighter than usual. The steeps were reflected in Brotherswater, and, above the lake appeared like enormous black perpendicular walls. The Kirkstone torrents had been swoln by the rain, and now filled the mountain pass with their roaring, which added greatly to the solemnity of our walk. Behind us, when we had climbed to a great height, we saw one light very distant in the vale, like a large red star—a solitary one in the gloomy region. The cheerfulness of the scene was in the sky above us. Reached home a little before midnight.

William Wordsworth.

Walking, and the Wild

I wish to speak a word for Nature, for absolute freedom and wildness, as contrasted with a freedom and culture merely civil,—to regard man as an inhabitant, or a part and parcel of Nature, rather than a member of society. I wish to make an extreme statement, if so I may make an emphatic one, for there are enough champions of civilisation: the minister and the school committee, and every one of you will take care of that.

I have met with but one or two persons in the course of my life who understood the art of Walking, that is, of taking walks,—who had a genius, so to speak, for *sauntering*: which word is beautifully derived "from idle people who roved about the country, in the Middle Ages, and asked charity, under pretence of going *à la Sainte Terre*," to the Holy Land, till the children exclaimed, "There goes a *Sainte-Terrer*," a Saunterer—a Holy-Lander. They who never go to the Holy Land in their walks, as they pretend, are indeed mere idlers and vagabonds; but they who do go there are saunterers in the good sense, such as I mean. Some, however, would derive the word from *sans terre*, without land or a home, which therefore, in the good sense, will mean, having no particular home, but equally at home everywhere. For this is the secret of successful sauntering. He who sits still in a house all the time may be the greatest vagrant of all; but the saunterer, in the good sense, is no more vagrant than the meandering river, which is all the while sedulously seeking the shortest course to the sea. But I prefer the first, which indeed is the most probable derivation. For every walk is a sort of crusade, preached by some Peter the Hermit in us, to go forth and reconquer this Holy Land from the hands of the Infidels.

It is true we are but faint-hearted crusaders, even the walkers, nowadays, who undertake no persevering, never-ending enterprises. Our expeditions are but tours, and come round again at evening to the old hearth-side from which we set out. Half the work is but retracing our steps. We should go forth on the shortest walk, perchance, in the spirit of undying adventure, never to return—prepared to send back our embalmed hearts only as relics to our desolate kingdoms. If you are ready to leave father and mother, and brother and sister, and wife and child and friends, and never see them again—if you have paid your debts, and made your will, and settled all your affairs, and are a free man, then you are ready for a walk.

To come down to my own experience, my companion and I, for I sometimes have a companion, take pleasure in fancying ourselves knights of a new, or rather an old, order—not Equestrians or Chevaliers, not Ritters or Riders, but Walkers, a still more ancient and honourable class, I trust. The chivalric and heroic spirit which once belonged to the Rider seems now to reside in, or perchance to have subsided into, the Walker,—not the Knight, but Walker Errant. He is a sort of fourth estate, outside of Church and State and People.

We have felt that we almost alone hereabouts practised this noble art; though, to tell the truth, at least if their own assertions are to be received, most of my townsmen would fain walk sometimes, as I do, but they cannot. No wealth can buy the requisite leisure, freedom, and independence, which are the capital in this profession. It comes only by the grace of God. It requires a direct dispensation from Heaven to become a walker. You must be born into the family of the Walkers. *Ambulator nascitur, non fit.* Some of my townsmen, it is true, can remember and have described to me some walks which they took ten years ago, in which they were so blessed as to lose themselves for half-an-hour in the woods; but I know very well that they have confined themselves to the highway ever since, whatever pretensions they may make to belong to this select class. No doubt they were elevated for a moment as by the reminiscence of a previous state of existence, when even they were foresters and outlaws.

> "When he came to grene wode,
> In a mery mornynge,
> There he herde the notes small
> Of byrdes mery syngynge.
>
> "It is ferre gone, sayd Robyn,
> That I was last here;
> Me lyste a lytell for to shote
> At the donne dere."

I think that I cannot preserve my health and spirits unless I spend four hours a day at least—and it is commonly more than that—sauntering through the woods and over the hills and fields, absolutely free from all worldly engagements. You may safely say, A penny for your thoughts, or a thousand pounds. When sometimes I am reminded that the mechanics and shopkeepers stay in their shops not only all the forenoon, but all the afternoon too, sitting with crossed legs, so many of them—as if the legs were made to sit upon, and not to stand or walk upon—I think that they deserve some credit for not having all committed suicide long ago.

I, who cannot stay in my chamber for a single day without acquiring some rust, and when sometimes I have stolen forth for a walk at the eleventh hour of four o'clock in the afternoon, too late to redeem the day, when the shades of night were already beginning to be mingled with the daylight, have felt as if I had committed some sin to be atoned for,—I confess that I am astonished at the power of endurance, to say nothing of the moral insensibility, of my neighbours who confine themselves to shops and offices the whole day for weeks and months, ay, and years almost together. I know not what manner of stuff they are of—sitting there now at three o'clock in the afternoon, as if it were three o'clock in the morning. Bonaparte may talk of the three-o'clock-in-the-morning courage, but it is nothing to the courage which can sit down cheerfully at this hour in the afternoon over against one's self whom you have known all the morning, to starve out a garrison to whom you are bound by such strong ties of sympathy. I wonder that about this time, or say between four and five o'clock in the afternoon, too late for the morning papers and too early for the evening ones, there is not a general explosion heard up and down the street, scattering a legion of antiquated and house-bred notions and whims to the four winds for an airing—and so the evil cure itself.

How womankind, who are confined to the house still more than men, stand it I do not know; but I have ground to suspect that most of them do not *stand* it at all. When, early in the summer afternoon, we have been shaking the dust of the village from the skirts of our garments, making haste past those houses with purely Doric or Gothic fronts, which have such an air of repose about them, my companion whispers that probably about these times their occupants are all gone to bed. Then it is that I appreciate the beauty and the glory of architecture, which itself never turns in, but for ever stands out and erect, keeping watch over the slumberers.

No doubt temperament, and, above all, age, have a good deal to do with it. As a man grows older, his ability to sit still and follow indoor occupations increases. He grows vespertinal in his habits as the evening of life approaches, till at last he comes forth only just before sundown, and gets all the walk that he requires in half-an-hour.

But the walking of which I speak has nothing in it akin to taking exercise, as it is called, as the sick take medicine at stated hours—as the swinging of dumb-bells or chairs; but is itself the enterprise and adventure of the day. If you would get exercise, go in search of the springs of life. Think of a man's swinging dumb-bells for his health, when those springs are bubbling up in far-off pastures unsought by him!

Moreover, you must walk like a camel, which is said to be the only beast which ruminates when walking. When a traveller asked Wordsworth's servant to show him her master's study, she answered, "Here is his library, but his study is out of doors."

Living much out of doors, in the sun and wind, will no doubt produce a certain roughness of character—will cause a thicker cuticle to grow over some of the finer qualities of our nature, as on the face and hands, or as severe manual labour robs the hands of some of their delicacy of touch. So staying in the house, on the other hand, may produce a softness and smoothness, not to say thinness of skin, accompanied by an increased sensibility to certain impressions. Perhaps we should be more susceptible to some influences important to our intellectual and moral growth if the sun had shone and the wind blown on us a little less; and no doubt it is a nice matter to proportion rightly the thick and thin skin. But methinks that is a scurf that will fall off fast enough—that the natural remedy is to be found in the proportion which the night bears to the day, the winter to the summer, thought to experience. There will be so much the more air and sunshine in our thoughts. The callous palms of the labourer are conversant with finer tissues of self-respect and heroism, whose touch thrills the heart, than the languid fingers of idleness. That is mere sentimentality that lies abed by day and thinks itself white, far from the tan and callus of experience.

When we walk, we naturally go to the fields and woods: what would become of us if we walked only in the garden or a mall? Even some sects of philosophers have felt the necessity of importing the woods to themselves, since they did not go to the woods. "They planted groves and walks of Platanes," where they took *subdiales ambulationes* in porticos open to the air. Of course it is of no use to direct our steps to the woods if they do not carry us thither. I am alarmed when it happens that I have walked a mile into the woods bodily without getting there in spirit. In my afternoon walk I would fain forget all my morning occupations and my obligations to society. But it sometimes happens that I cannot easily shake off the village. The thought of some work will run in my head, and I am not where my body is—I am out of my senses. In my walks I would fain return to my senses. What business have I in the woods, if I am thinking of something out of the woods? I suspect myself, and cannot help a shudder, when I find myself so implicated even in what are called good works—for this may sometimes happen.

My vicinity affords many good walks; and though for so many years I have walked almost every day, and sometimes for several days together, I have not yet exhausted them. An absolutely new prospect is a great happiness, and I can still get this any afternoon. Two or three hours' walking will carry me to as strange a country as I expect ever to see. A single farmhouse which I had not seen before is sometimes as good as the dominions of the King of Dahomey. There is in fact a sort of harmony discoverable between the capabilities of the landscape within a circle of ten miles' radius, or the limits of an afternoon walk, and the threescore years and ten of human life. It will never become quite familiar to you.

Nowadays almost all man's improvements, so called, as the building of houses, and the cutting down of the forest and of all large trees, simply deform the landscape, and make it more and more tame and cheap. A people who would begin by burning the fences and let the forest stand! I saw the fences half consumed, their ends lost in the middle of the prairie, and some worldly miser with a surveyor looking after his bounds, while heaven had taken place around him, and he did not see the angels going to and fro, but was looking for an old posthole in the midst of paradise. I looked again, and saw him standing in the middle of a boggy, stygian fen, surrounded by devils, and he had found his bounds without a doubt, three little stones, where a stake had been driven, and looking nearer, I saw that the Prince of Darkness was his surveyor.

I can easily walk ten, fifteen, twenty, any number of miles, commencing at my own door, without going by any house, without crossing a road except where the fox and the mink do: first along by the river, and then the brook, and then the meadow and the woodside. There are square miles in my vicinity which have no inhabitant. From many a hill I can see civilisation and the abodes of man afar. The farmers and their works are scarcely more obvious than woodchucks and their burrows. Man and his affairs, church and state and school, trade and commerce, and manufactures and agriculture, even politics, the most alarming of them all,—I am pleased to see how little space they occupy in the landscape. Politics is but a narrow field, and that still narrower highway yonder leads to it. I sometimes direct the traveller thither. If you would go to the political world, follow the great road—follow that market-man, keep his dust in your eyes, and it will lead you straight to it; for it, too, has its place merely, and does not occupy all space. I pass from it as from a beanfield into the forest, and it is forgotten. In one half-hour I can walk off to some portion of the earth's surface where a man does not stand from one year's end to another and there, consequently, politics are not, for they are but as the cigar-smoke of a man.

The village is the place to which the roads tend, a sort of expansion of the highway, as a lake of a river. It is the body of which roads are the arms and legs—a trivial or quadrivial place, the thoroughfare and ordinary of travellers. The word is from the Latin *villa*, which, together with *via*, a way, or more anciently *ved* and *vella*, Varro derives from *veho*, to carry, because the villa is the place to and from which things are carried. They who get their living by teaming were said *vellaturam facere*. Hence, too, apparently, the Latin word *vilis* and our vile; also *villain*. This suggests what kind of degeneracy villagers are liable to. They are wayworn by the travel that goes by and over them, without travelling themselves.

Some do not walk at all; others walk in the highways; a few walk across lots. Roads are made for horses and men of business. I do not travel in them much, comparatively, because I am not in a hurry to get to any tavern or grocery or livery-stable or depôt to which they lead. I am a good horse to travel, but not from choice a roadster. The landscape-painter uses the figures of men to mark a road. He would not make that use of my figure. I walk out into a Nature such as the old prophets and poets, Menu, Moses, Homer, Chaucer, walked in. You may name it America, but it is not America: neither Americus Vespucius, nor Columbus, nor the rest were the discoverers of it. There is a truer account of it in mythology than in any history of America, so called, that I have seen.

At present, in this vicinity, the best part of the land is not private property; the landscape is not owned, and the walker enjoys comparative freedom. But possibly the day will come when it will be partitioned off into so-called pleasure-grounds, in which a few will take a narrow and exclusive pleasure only,—when fences shall be multiplied, and mantraps and other engines invented to confine men to the *public road*, and walking over the surface of God's earth shall be construed to mean trespassing on some gentleman's grounds. To enjoy a thing exclusively is commonly to exclude yourself from the true enjoyment of it. Let us improve our opportunities, then, before the evil days come.

What is it that makes it so hard sometimes to determine whither we will walk? I believe that there is a subtle magnetism in Nature which, if we unconsciously yield to it, will direct us aright. It is not indifferent to us which way we walk. There is a right way; but we are very liable from heedlessness and stupidity to take the wrong one. We would fain take that walk, never yet taken by us through this actual world, which is perfectly symbolical of the path which we love to travel in the interior and ideal world; and sometimes, no doubt, we find it difficult to choose our direction, because it does not yet exist distinctly in our idea.

When I go out of the house for a walk, uncertain as yet whither I will bend my steps, and submit myself to my instinct to decide for me, I find, strange and whimsical as it may seem, that I finally and inevitably settle south-west, toward some particular wood or meadow or deserted pasture or hill in that direction. My needle is slow to settle,—varies a few degrees, and does not always point due south-west, it is true, and it has good authority for this variation, but it always settles between west and south-south-west. The future lies that way to me, and the earth seems more unexhausted and richer on that side. The outline which would bound my walks would be, not a circle, but a parabola, or rather like one of those cometary orbits which have been thought to be non-returning curves, in this case opening westward, in which my house occupies the place of the sun. I turn round and round irresolute, sometimes for a quarter of an hour, until I decide, for a thousandth time, that I will walk into the south-west or west. Eastward I go only by force; but westward I go free. Thither no business leads me. It is hard for me to believe that I shall find fair landscapes or sufficient wildness and freedom behind the eastern horizon. I am not excited by the prospect of a walk thither; but I believe that the forest which I see in the western horizon stretches uninterruptedly toward the setting sun, and there are no towns nor cities in it of enough consequence to disturb me. Let me live where I will, on this side is the city, on that the wilderness, and ever I am leaving the city more and more, and withdrawing into the wilderness. I should not lay so much stress on this fact, if I did not believe that something like this is the prevailing tendency of my countrymen. I must walk toward Oregon, and not toward Europe. And that way the nation is moving, and I may say that mankind progress from east to west. Within a few years we have witnessed the phenomenon of a south-eastward migration in the settlement of Australia; but this affects us as a retrograde movement, and, judging from the moral and physical character of the first generation of Australians, has not yet proved a successful experiment. The eastern Tartars think that there is nothing west beyond Thibet. "The world ends there," say they; "beyond there is nothing but a shoreless sea." It is unmitigated East where they live.

We go eastward to realise history and study the works of art and literature, retracing the steps of the race; we go westward as into the future, with a spirit of enterprise and adventure. The Atlantic is a Lethean stream, in our passage over which we have had an opportunity to forget the Old World and its institutions. If we do not succeed this time, there is perhaps one more chance for the race left before it arrives on the banks of the Styx; and that is in the Lethe of the Pacific, which is three times as wide.

I know not how significant it is, or how far it is an evidence of singularity, that an individual should thus consent in his pettiest walk with the general movement of the race; but I know that something akin to the migratory instinct in birds and quadrupeds,— which, in some instances, is known to have affected the squirrel tribe, impelling them to a general and mysterious movement, in which they were seen, say some, crossing the broadest rivers, each on its particular chip, with its tail raised for a sail, and bridging narrower streams with their dead,—that something like a *furor* which affects the domestic cattle in the spring, and which is referred to a worm in their tails,—affects both nations and individuals, either perennially or from time to time. Not a flock of wild geese cackles over our town, but it to some extent unsettles the value of real estate here, and, if I were a broker, I should probably take that disturbance into account.

> "Than longen folk to gon on pilgrimages,
> And palmeres for to seken strange strondes."

Every sunset which I witness inspires me with the desire to go to a West as distant and as fair as that into which the sun goes down. He appears to migrate westward daily, and tempts us to follow him. He is the Great Western Pioneer whom the nations follow. We dream all night of those mountain-ridges in the horizon, though they may be of vapour only, which were last gilded by his rays. The islands of

Atlantis, and the islands and gardens of the Hesperides, a sort of terrestrial paradise, appear to have been the Great West of the ancients, enveloped in mystery and poetry. Who has not seen in imagination, when looking into the sunset sky, the gardens of the Hesperides, and the foundation of all those fables?

Columbus felt the westward tendency more strongly than any before. He obeyed it, and found a New World for Castile and Leon. The head of men in those days scented fresh pastures from afar.

> "And now the sun had stretched out all the hills,
> And now was dropped into the western bay;
> At last *he* rose, and twitched his mantle blue;
> To-morrow to fresh woods and pastures new."

Where on the globe can there be found an area of equal extent with that occupied by the bulk of our States, so fertile and so rich and varied in its proportions, and at the same time so habitable by the European, as this is? Michaux, who knew but part of them, says that "the species of large trees are much more numerous in North America than in Europe; in the United States there are more than one hundred and forty species that exceed thirty feet in height; in France there are but thirty that attain this size." Later botanists more than confirm his observations. Humboldt came to America to realise his youthful dreams of a tropical vegetation, and he beheld it in its greatest perfection in the primitive forests of the Amazon, the most gigantic wilderness on the earth, which he has so eloquently described. The geographer Guyot, himself a European, goes farther—farther than I am ready to follow him; yet not when he says: "As the plant is made for the animal, as the vegetable world is made for the animal world, America is made for the man of the Old World.... The man of the Old World sets out upon his way. Leaving the highlands of Asia, he descends from station to station towards Europe. Each of his steps is marked by a new civilisation superior to the preceding, by a greater power of development. Arrived at the Atlantic, he pauses on the shore of this unknown ocean, the bounds of which he knows not, and turns upon his footprints for an instant." When he has exhausted the rich soil of Europe, and reinvigorated himself, "then recommences his adventurous career westward as in the earliest ages." So far Guyot.

From this western impulse coming in contact with the barrier of the Atlantic sprang the commerce and enterprise of modern times. The younger Michaux, in his *Travels West of the Alleghanies in 1802*, says that the common inquiry in the newly settled West was, "'From what part of the world have you come?' As if these vast and fertile regions would naturally be the place of meeting and common country of all the inhabitants of the globe."

To use an obsolete Latin word, I might say, *Ex Oriente lux; ex Occidente* FRUX. From the East light; from the West fruit.

Sir Francis Head, an English traveller and a Governor-General of Canada, tells us that "in both the northern and southern hemispheres of the New World, Nature has not only outlined her words on a larger scale, but has painted the whole picture with brighter and more costly colours than she used in delineating and in beautifying the Old World.... The heavens of America appear infinitely higher, the sky is bluer, the air is fresher, the cold is intenser, the moon looks larger, the stars are brighter, the thunder is louder, the lightning is vivider, the wind is stronger, the rain is heavier, the mountains are higher, the rivers longer, the forests bigger, the plains broader." This statement will do at least to set against Buffon's account of this part of the world and its productions.

Linnæus said long ago, "*Nescio quæ facies* læta, glabra *plantis Americanis*: I know not what there is of joyous and smooth in the aspect of American plants"; and I think that in this country there are no, or at most very few, *Africanæ bestiæ*, African beasts, as the Romans called them, and that in this respect also it is peculiarly fitted for the habitation of man. We are told that within three miles of the centre of the East Indian city of Singapore, some of the inhabitants are annually carried off by tigers; but the traveller can lie down in the woods at night almost anywhere in North America without fear of wild beasts.

These are encouraging testimonies. If the moon looks larger here than in Europe, probably the sun looks larger also. If the heavens of America appear infinitely higher, and the stars brighter, I trust that these facts are symbolical of the height to which the philosophy and poetry and religion of her inhabitants may one day soar. At length, perchance, the immaterial heaven will appear as much higher to the American mind, and the intimations that star it as much brighter. For I believe that climate does thus react on man—as there is something in the mountain air that feeds the spirit and inspires. Will not man grow to greater perfection intellectually as well as physically under these influences? Or is it unimportant how many foggy days there are in his life? I trust that we shall be more imaginative, that our thoughts will be clearer, fresher, and more ethereal, as our sky—our understanding more comprehensive and broader, like our plains—our intellect generally on a grander scale, like our thunder and lightning, our rivers and mountains and forests—and our hearts shall even correspond in breadth and depth and grandeur to our inland seas. Perchance there will appear to the traveller something, he knows not what, of *læta* and *glabra*, of joyous and serene, in our very faces. Else to what end does the world go on, and why was America discovered?

To Americans I hardly need to say:

"Westward the star of empire takes its way."

As a true patriot, I should be ashamed to think that Adam in paradise was more favourably situated on the whole than the backwoodsman in this country.

Our sympathies in Massachusetts are not confined to New England; though we may be estranged from the South, we sympathise with the West. There is the home of the younger sons, as among the Scandinavians they took to the sea for their inheritance. It is too late to be studying Hebrew; it is more important to understand even the slang of to-day.

Some months ago I went to see a panorama of the Rhine. It was like a dream of the Middle Ages. I floated down its historic stream in something more than imagination, under bridges built by the Romans, and repaired by later heroes, past cities and castles whose very names were music to my ears, and each of which was the subject of a legend. There were Ehrenbreitstein and Rolandseck and Coblentz, which I knew only in history. They were ruins that interested me chiefly. There seemed to come up from its waters and its vine-clad hills and valleys a hushed music as of Crusaders departing for the Holy Land. I floated along under the spell of enchantment, as if I had been transported to an heroic age, and breathed an atmosphere of chivalry.

Soon after I went to see a panorama of the Mississippi, and as I worked my way up the river in the light of to-day, and saw the steamboats wooding up, counted the rising cities, gazed on the fresh ruins of Nauvoo, beheld the Indians moving west across the stream, and, as before I had looked up the Moselle, now looked up the Ohio and the Missouri and heard the legends of Dubuque and of Wenona's Cliff,—still thinking more of the future than of the past or present,—I saw that this was a Rhine stream of a different kind; that the foundations of castles were yet to be laid, and the famous bridges were yet to be thrown over the river; and I felt that *this was the heroic age itself*, though we know it not, for the hero is commonly the simplest and obscurest of men.

The West of which I speak is but another name for the Wild; and what I have been preparing to say is, that in Wildness is the preservation of the World. Every tree sends its fibres forth in search of the Wild. The cities import it at any price. Men plough and sail for it. From the forest and wilderness come the tonics and barks which brace mankind. Our ancestors were savages. The story of Romulus and Remus being suckled by a wolf is not a meaningless fable. The founders of every State which has risen to eminence have drawn their nourishment and vigour from a similar wild source. It was because the children of the Empire were not suckled by the wolf that they were conquered and displaced by the children of the Northern forests who were.

I believe in the forest, and in the meadow, and in the night in which the corn grows. We require an infusion of hemlock-spruce or arborvitæ in our tea. There is a difference between eating and drinking for strength and from mere gluttony. The Hottentots eagerly devour the marrow of the koodoo and other antelopes raw, as a matter of course. Some of our Northern Indians eat raw the marrow of the Arctic reindeer, as well as various other parts, including the summits of the antlers, as long as they are soft. And herein, perchance, they have stolen a march on the cooks of Paris. They get what usually goes to feed the fire. This is probably better than stall-fed beef and slaughter-house pork to make a man of. Give me a wildness whose glance no civilisation can endure,—as if we lived on the marrow of koodoos devoured raw.

There are some intervals which border the strain of the wood-thrush, to which I would migrate,—wild lands where no settler has squatted; to which, methinks, I am already acclimated.

The African hunter Cummings tells us that the skin of the eland, as well as that of most other antelopes just killed, emits the most delicious perfume of trees and grass. I would have every man so much like a wild antelope, so much a part and parcel of Nature, that his very person should thus sweetly advertise our senses of his presence, and remind us of those parts of Nature which he most haunts. I feel no disposition to be satirical, when the trapper's coat emits the odour of musquash even; it is a sweeter scent to me than that which commonly exhales from the merchant's or the scholar's garments. When I go into their wardrobes and handle their vestments, I am reminded of no grassy plains and flowery meads which they have frequented, but of dusty merchants' exchanges and libraries rather.

A tanned skin is something more than respectable, and perhaps olive is a fitter colour than white for a man—a denizen of the woods. "The pale white man!" I do not wonder that the African pitied him. Darwin the naturalist says, "A white man bathing by the side of a Tahitian was like a plant bleached by the gardener's art, compared with a fine, dark green one, growing vigorously in the open fields."

Ben Jonson exclaims:

"How near to good is what is fair!"

So I would say:

How near to good is what is *wild*!

Life consists with wildness. The most alive is the wildest. Not yet subdued to man, its presence refreshes him. One who pressed forward incessantly and never rested from his labours, who grew fast and made infinite demands on life, would always find himself in a new country or wilderness, and surrounded by the raw material of life. He would be climbing over the prostrate stems of primitive forest trees.

Hope and the future for me are not in lawns and cultivated fields, not in towns and cities, but in the impervious and quaking swamps. When, formerly, I have analysed my partiality for some farm which I had contemplated purchasing, I have frequently found that I was attracted solely by a few square rods of impermeable and unfathomable bog—a natural sink in one corner of it. That was the jewel which dazzled me. I derive more of my subsistence from the swamps which surround my native town than from the cultivated gardens in the village. There are no richer parterres to my eyes than the dense beds of dwarf andromeda (*Cassandra calyculata*) which cover these tender places on the earth's surface. Botany cannot go further than tell me the names of the shrubs which grow there—the high-blueberry, panicled andromeda, lambkill, azalea, and rhodora—all standing in the quaking sphagnum. I often think that I should like to have my house front on this mass of dull red bushes, omitting other flower plots and borders, transplanted spruce and trim box, even gravelled walks—to have this fertile spot under my windows, not a few imported barrowfuls of soil only to cover the sand which was thrown out in digging the cellar. Why not put my house, my parlour, behind this plot, instead of behind that meagre assemblage of curiosities, that poor apology for a Nature and Art which I call my front yard? It is an effort to clear up and make a decent appearance when the carpenter and mason have departed, though done as much for the passer-by as the dweller within. The most tasteful front-yard fence was never an agreeable object of study to me; the most elaborate ornaments, acorn-tops, or what not, soon wearied and disgusted me. Bring your sills up to the very edge of the swamp, then (though it may not be the best place for a dry cellar), so that there be no access on that side to citizens. Front yards are not made to walk in, but, at most, through, and you could go in the back way.

Yes, though you may think me perverse, if it were proposed to me to dwell in the neighbourhood of the most beautiful garden that ever human art contrived, or else of a dismal swamp, I should certainly decide for the swamp. How vain, then, have been all your labours, citizens, for me!

My spirits infallibly rise in proportion to the outward dreariness. Give me the ocean, the desert or the wilderness! In the desert, pure air and solitude compensate for want of moisture and fertility. The traveller Burton says of it—"Your *morale* improves; you become frank and cordial, hospitable and single-minded.... In the desert, spirituous liquors excite only disgust. There is a keen enjoyment in a mere animal existence." They who have been travelling long on the steppes of Tartary say—"On re-entering cultivated lands, the agitation, perplexity, and turmoil of civilisation oppressed and suffocated us; the air seemed to fail us, and we felt every moment as if about to die of asphyxia." When I would recreate myself, I seek the darkest wood, the thickest and most interminable, and, to the citizen, most dismal swamp. I enter a swamp as a sacred place,—*a sanctum sanctorum*. There is the strength, the marrow of Nature. The wild-wood covers the virgin mould,—and the same soil is good for men and for trees. A man's health requires as many acres of meadow to his prospect as his farm does loads of muck. There are the strong meats on which he feeds. A town is saved, not more by the righteous men in it than by the woods and swamps that surround it. A township where one primitive forest waves above while another primitive forest rots below,—such a town is fitted to raise not only corn and potatoes, but poets and philosophers for the coming ages. In such a soil grew Homer and Confucius and the rest, and out of such a wilderness comes the Reformer eating locusts and wild honey.

To preserve wild animals implies generally the creation of a forest for them to dwell in or resort to. So it is with man. A hundred years ago they sold bark in our streets peeled from our own woods. In the very aspect of those primitive and rugged trees there was, methinks, a tanning principle which hardened and consolidated the fibres of men's thoughts. Ah! already I shudder for these comparatively degenerate days of my native village, when you cannot collect a load of bark of good thickness; and we no longer produce tar and turpentine.

The civilised nations—Greece, Rome, England—have been sustained by the primitive forests which anciently rotted where they stand. They survive as long as the soil is not exhausted. Alas for human culture! little is to be expected of a nation when the vegetable mould is exhausted, and it is compelled to make manure of the bones of its fathers. There the poet sustains himself merely by his own superfluous fat, and the philosopher comes down on his marrow-bones.

It is said to be the task of the American "to work the virgin soil," and that "agriculture here already assumes proportions unknown everywhere else." I think that the farmer displaces the Indian even because he redeems the meadow, and so makes himself stronger and in some respects more natural. I was surveying for a man the other day a single straight line one hundred and thirty-two rods long, through a swamp, at whose entrance might have been written the words which Dante read over the entrance to the infernal regions—"Leave all hope, ye that enter,"—that is, of ever getting out again; where at one time I saw my employer actually up to his neck and swimming for his life in his property, though it was still winter. He had another similar swamp which I could not survey at all, because it was completely under water; and nevertheless, with regard to a third swamp, which I did *survey* from a distance, he remarked to me, true to his instincts, that he would not part with it for any consideration, on account of the mud which it contained. And that man intends to put a girdling ditch round the whole in the course of forty months, and so redeem it by the magic of his spade. I refer to him only as the type of a class.

The weapons with which we have gained our most important victories, which should be handed down as heirlooms from father to son, are not the sword and the lance, but the bush-whack, the turf cutter, the spade, and the bog-hoe, rusted with the blood of many a meadow, and begrimed with the dust of many a hard-fought field. The very winds blew the Indian's corn-field into the meadow, and pointed out the way which he had not the skill to follow. He had no better implement with which to intrench himself in the land than a clamshell. But the farmer is armed with plough and spade.

In Literature it is only the wild that attracts us. Dullness is but another name for tameness. It is the uncivilised free and wild thinking in *Hamlet* and the *Iliad*, in all the Scriptures and Mythologies, not learned in the schools, that delights us. As the wild duck is more swift and beautiful than the tame, so is the wild—the mallard—thought, which 'mid falling dews wings its way above the fens. A truly good book is something as natural, and as unexpectedly and unaccountably fair and perfect, as a wild flower discovered on the prairies of the West or in the jungles of the East. Genius is a light which makes the darkness visible, like the lightning's flash, which perchance shatters the temple of knowledge itself,—and not a taper lighted at the hearth-stone of the race, which pales before the light of common day.

English literature, from the days of the minstrels to the Lake Poets—Chaucer and Spenser and Milton, and even Shakespeare, included—breathes no quite fresh and in this sense wild strain. It is an essentially tame and civilised literature, reflecting Greece and Rome. Her wilderness is a green wood,—her wild man a Robin Hood. There is plenty of genial love of Nature, but not so much of Nature herself. Her chronicles inform us when her wild animals, but not when the wild man in her, became extinct.

The science of Humboldt is one thing, poetry is another thing. The poet to-day, notwithstanding all the discoveries of science, and the accumulated learning of mankind, enjoys no advantage over Homer.

Where is the literature which gives expression to Nature? He would be a poet who could impress the winds and streams into his service, to speak for him; who nailed words to their primitive senses, as farmers drive down stakes in the spring, which the frost has heaved; who derived his words as often as he used them—transplanted them to his page with earth adhering to their roots; whose words were so true and fresh and natural that they would appear to expand like the buds at the approach of spring, though they lay half-smothered between two musty leaves in a library,—ay, to bloom and bear fruit there, after their kind, annually, for the faithful reader, in sympathy with surrounding Nature.

I do not know of any poetry to quote which adequately expresses this yearning for the Wild. Approached from this side, the best poetry is tame. I do not know where to find in any literature, ancient or modern, any account which contents me of that Nature with which even I am acquainted. You will perceive that I demand something which no Augustan nor Elizabethan age, which no *culture*, in short, can give. Mythology comes nearer to it than anything. How much more fertile a Nature, at least, has Grecian mythology its root in than English literature. Mythology is the crop which the Old World bore before its soil was exhausted, before the fancy and imagination were affected with blight; and, which it still bears, whenever its pristine vigour is unabated. All other literatures endure only as the elms which overshadow our houses; but this is like the great dragon-tree of the Western Isles, as old as mankind, and, whether that does or not, will endure as long; for the decay of other literatures makes the soil in which it thrives.

The West is preparing to add its fables to those of the East. The valleys of the Ganges, the Nile, and the Rhine, having yielded their crop, it remains to be seen what the valleys of the Amazon, the Plate, the Orinoco, the St Lawrence, and the Mississippi will produce. Perchance, when, in the course of ages, American liberty has become a fiction of the past—as it is to some extent a fiction of the present—the poets of the world will be inspired by American mythology.

The wildest dreams of wild men, even, are not the less true, though they may not recommend themselves to the sense which is most common among Englishmen and Americans to-day. It is not every truth that recommends itself to the common sense. Nature has a place for the wild clematis as well as for the cabbage. Some expressions of truth are reminiscent,—others merely *sensible*, as the phrase is,—others prophetic. Some forms of disease, even, may prophesy forms of health. The geologist has discovered that the figures of serpents, griffins, flying dragons, and other fanciful embellishments of heraldry, have their prototypes in the forms of fossil species which were extinct before man was created, and hence "indicate a faint and shadowy knowledge of a previous state of organic existence." The Hindoos dreamed that the earth rested on an elephant, and the elephant on a tortoise, and the tortoise on a serpent; and though it may be an unimportant coincidence, it will not be out of place here to state that a fossil tortoise has lately been discovered in Asia large enough to support an elephant. I confess that I am partial to these wild fancies, which transcend the order of time and development. They are the sublimest recreation of the intellect. The partridge loves peas, but not those that go with her into the pot.

In short, all good things are wild and free There is something in a strain of music, whether produced by an instrument or by the human voice,—take the sound of a bugle in a summer night for instance,—which by its wildness, to speak without satire, reminds me of the cries emitted by wild beasts in their native forests. It is so much of their wildness as I can understand. Give me for my friends and neighbours wild men, not tame ones. The wilderness of the savage is but a faint symbol of the awful ferity with which good men and lovers meet.

I love even to see the domestic animals reassert their native rights,—any evidence that they have not wholly lost their original wild habits and vigour; as when my neighbour's cow breaks out of her pasture early in the spring and boldly swims the river, a cold, grey tide, twenty-five or thirty rods wide, swollen by the melted snow. It is the buffalo crossing the Mississippi. This exploit confers some dignity on the herd of my eyes—already dignified. The seeds of instinct are preserved under the thick hides of cattle and horses, like seeds in the bowels of the earth, an indefinite period.

Any sportiveness in cattle is unexpected. I saw one day a herd of a dozen bullocks and cows running about and frisking in unwieldy sport, like huge rats, even like kittens. They shook their heads, raised their tails, and rushed up and down a hill, and I perceived by their horns, as well as by their activity, their relation to the deer tribe. But, alas! a sudden loud *Whoa!* would have damped their ardour at once, reduced them from venison to beef, and stiffened their sides and sinews like the locomotive. Who but the Evil One has cried, "Whoa!" to mankind? Indeed, the life of cattle, like that of many men, is but a sort of locomotiveness; they move a side at a time, and man, by his machinery, is meeting the horse and the ox half way. Whatever part the whip has touched is thenceforth palsied. Who would ever think of a *side* of any of the supple cat tribe, as we speak of a *side* of beef?

I rejoice that horses and steers have to be broken before they can be made the slaves of men, and that men themselves have some wild oats still left to sow before they become submissive members of society. Undoubtedly, all men are not equally fit subjects for civilisation; and because the majority, like dogs and sheep, are tame by inherited disposition, this is no reason why the others should have their natures broken that they may be reduced to the same level. Men are in the main alike, but they were made several in order that they might be various. If a low use is to be served, one man will do nearly or quite as well as another; if a high one, individual excellence is to be regarded. Any man can stop a hole to keep the wind away, but no other man could serve so rare a use as the author of this illustration did. Confucius says—"The skins of the tiger and the leopard, when they are tanned, are as the skins of the dog and the sheep tanned." But it is not the part of a true culture to tame tigers, any more than it is to make sheep ferocious; and tanning their skins for shoes is not the best use to which they can be put.

When looking over a list of men's names in a foreign language, as of military officers, or of authors who have written on a particular subject, I am reminded once more that there is nothing in a name. The name Menschikoff, for instance, has nothing in it to my ears more human than a whisker, and it may belong to a rat. As the names of the Poles and Russians are to us, so are ours to them. It is as if they had been named by the child's rigmarole—*Iery wiery ichery van, tittle-tol-tan*. I see in my mind a herd of wild creatures swarming over the earth, and to each the herdsman has affixed some barbarous sound in his own dialect. The names of men are of course as cheap and as meaningless as *Bose* and *Tray*, the names of dogs.

Methinks it would be some advantage to philosophy if men were named merely in the gross, as they are known. It would be necessary only to know the genus, and perhaps the race or variety, to know the individual. We are not prepared to believe that every private soldier in a Roman army had a name of his own, because we have not supposed that he had a character of his own. At present, our only true names are nicknames. I knew a boy who, from his peculiar energy, was called "Buster" by his playmates, and this rightly supplanted his Christian name. Some travellers tell us that an Indian had no name given him at first, but earned it, and his name was his fame; and among some tribes he acquired a new name with every new exploit. It is pitiful when a man bears a name for convenience merely, who has earned neither name nor fame.

I will not allow mere names to make distinctions for me, but still see men in herds for all them. A familiar name cannot make a man less strange to me. It may be given to a savage who retains in secret his own wild title earned in the woods. We have a wild savage in us, and a savage name is perchance somewhere recorded as ours. I see that my neighbour, who bears the familiar epithet William, or Edwin, takes it off with his jacket. It does not adhere to him when asleep or in anger, or aroused by any passion or inspiration. I seem to hear pronounced by some of his kin at such a time his original wild name in some jaw-breaking or else melodious tongue.

Here is this vast, savage, howling mother of ours, Nature, lying all around, with such beauty, and such affection for her children, as the leopard; and yet we are so early weaned from her breast to society, to that culture which is exclusively an interaction of man on man—a sort of breeding in and in, which produces at most a merely English nobility, a civilisation destined to have a speedy limit.

In society, in the best institutions of men, it is easy to detect a certain precocity. When we should still be growing children, we are already little men. Give me a culture which imports much muck from the meadows, and deepens the soil—not that which trusts to heating manures and improved implements and modes of culture only.

Many a poor sore-eyed student that I have heard of would grow faster, both intellectually and physically, if, instead of sitting up so very late, he honestly slumbered a fool's allowance.

There may be an excess even of informing light. Niépce, a Frenchman, discovered "actinism," that power in the sun's rays which produces a chemical effect,—that granite rocks, and stone structures, and statues of metal, "are all alike destructively acted upon during the hours of sunshine, and, but for provisions of Nature no less wonderful, would soon perish under the delicate touch of the most subtile of the agencies of the universe." But he observed that "those bodies which underwent this change during the daylight possessed the power of restoring themselves to their original conditions during the hours of night, when this excitement was no longer influencing them." Hence it has been inferred that "the hours of darkness are as necessary to the creation as we know night and sleep are to the organic kingdom." Not even does the moon shine every night, but gives place to darkness.

I would not have every man nor every part of man cultivated, any more than I would have every acre of earth cultivated: part will be tillage, but the greater part will be meadow and forest, not only serving an immediate use, but preparing a mould against a distant future, by the annual decay of the vegetation which it supports.

There are other letters for the child to learn than those which Cadmus invented. The Spaniards have a good term to express this wild and dusky knowledge,—*Gramática parda*, tawny grammar,—a kind of mother-wit derived from that same leopard to which I have referred.

We have heard of a Society for the Diffusion of Useful Knowledge. It is said that knowledge is power; and the like. Methinks there is equal need of a Society for the Diffusion of Useful Ignorance, what we will call Beautiful Knowledge, a knowledge useful in a higher sense: for what is most of our boasted so-called knowledge but a conceit that we know something, which robs us of the advantage of our actual ignorance? What we call knowledge is often our positive ignorance; ignorance our negative knowledge. By long years of patient industry and reading of the newspapers—for what are the libraries of science but files of newspapers?—a man accumulates a myriad facts, lays them up in his memory, and then when in some spring of his life he saunters abroad into the Great Fields of thought, he, as it were, goes to grass like a horse and leaves all his harness behind in the stable. I would say to the Society for the Diffusion of Useful Knowledge, sometimes,—Go to grass. You have eaten hay long enough. The spring has come with its green crop. The very cows are driven to their country pastures before the end of May; though I have heard of one unnatural farmer who kept his cow in the barn and fed her on hay all the year round. So, frequently, the Society for the Diffusion of Useful Knowledge treats its cattle.

A man's ignorance sometimes is not only useful, but beautiful,— while his knowledge, so called, is oftentimes worse than useless, besides being ugly. Which is the best man to deal with—he who knows nothing about a subject, and, what is extremely rare, knows that he knows nothing, or he who really knows something about it, but thinks that he knows all?

My desire for knowledge is intermittent; but my desire to bathe my head in atmospheres unknown to my feet is perennial and constant. The highest that we can attain to is not Knowledge, but Sympathy with Intelligence. I do not know that this higher knowledge amounts to anything more definite than a novel and grand surprise on a sudden revelation of the insufficiency of all that we called Knowledge before—a discovery that there are more things in heaven and earth than are dreamed of in our philosophy. It is the lighting up of the mist by the sun. Man cannot *know* in any higher sense than this, any more than he can look serenely and with impunity in the face of the sun: Ως τι νοων κεινον νοήσεις [Greek: Hôs ti noôn ny keinon noêseis],—"You will not perceive that, as perceiving a particular thing," say the Chaldean Oracles.

There is something servile in the habit of seeking after a law which we may obey. We may study the laws of matter at and for our convenience, but a successful life knows no law. It is an unfortunate discovery certainly, that of a law which binds us where we did not know before that we were bound. Live free, child of the mist,—and with respect to knowledge we are all children of the mist. The man who takes the liberty to live is superior to all the laws, by virtue of his relation to the law-maker. "That is active duty," says the Vishnu Purana, "which is not for our bondage; that is knowledge which is for our liberation: all other duty is good only unto weariness; all other knowledge is only the cleverness of an artist."

It is remarkable how few events or crises there are in our histories; how little exercised we have been in our minds; how few experiences we have had. I would fain be assured that I am growing apace and rankly, though my very growth disturb this dull equanimity,—though it be with struggle through long, dark, muggy nights or seasons of gloom. It would be well if all our lives were a divine tragedy even, instead of this trivial comedy or farce. Dante, Bunyan, and others, appear to have been exercised in their minds more than we: they were subjected to a kind of culture such as our district schools and colleges do not contemplate. Even Mahomet, though many may scream at his name, had a good deal more to live for, ay, and to die for, than they have commonly.

When, at rare intervals, some thought visits one, as perchance he is walking on a railroad, then indeed the cars go by without his hearing them. But soon, by some inexorable law, our life goes by and the cars return.

> "Gentle breeze, that wanderest unseen,
> And bendest the thistles round Loira of storms,
> Traveller of the windy glens,
> Why hast thou left my ear so soon?"

While almost all men feel an attraction drawing them to society, few are attracted strongly to Nature. In their relation to Nature men appear to me for the most part, notwithstanding their arts, lower than the animals. It is not often a beautiful relation, as in the case of the animals. How little appreciation of the beauty of the landscape there is among us! We shall have to be told that the Greeks called the world Κόσμος [Greek: Kosmos], Beauty, or Order, but we do not see clearly why they did so, and we esteem it at best only a curious philological fact.

For my part, I feel that with regard to Nature I live a sort of border life, on the confines of a world into which I make occasional and transitional and transient forays only, and my patriotism and allegiance to the State into whose territories I seem to retreat are those of a moss-trooper. Unto a life which I call natural I would gladly follow even a will-o'-the wisp through bogs and sloughs unimaginable, but no moon nor fire-fly has shown me the causeway to it. Nature is a personality so vast and universal that we have never seen one of her features. The walker in the familiar fields which stretch around my native town sometimes finds himself in another land than is described in their owners' deeds, as it were in some far-away field on the confines of the actual Concord, where her jurisdiction ceases, and the idea which the word Concord suggests ceases to be suggested. These farms which I have myself surveyed, these bounds which I have set up, appear dimly still as through a mist; but they have no chemistry to fix them; they fade from the surface of the glass; and the picture which the painter painted stands out dimly from beneath. The world with which we are commonly acquainted leaves no trace, and it will have no anniversary.

I took a walk on Spaulding's Farm the other afternoon. I saw the setting sun lighting up the opposite side of a stately pine wood. Its golden rays straggled into the aisles of the wood as into some noble hall. I was impressed as if some ancient and altogether admirable and shining family had settled there in that part of the land called Concord, unknown to me,—to whom the sun was servant,—who had not gone into society in the village,—who had not been called on. I saw their park, their pleasure-ground, beyond through the wood, in

Spaulding's cranberry-meadow. The pines furnished them with gables as they grew. Their house was not obvious to vision; the trees grew through it. I do not know whether I heard the sounds of a suppressed hilarity or not. They seemed to recline on the sunbeams. They have sons and daughters. They are quite well. The farmer's cart-path, which leads directly through their hall, does not in the least put them out,—as the muddy bottom of a pool is sometimes seen through the reflected skies. They never heard of Spaulding, and do not know that he is their neighbour,—notwithstanding I heard him whistle as he drove his team through the house. Nothing can equal the serenity of their lives. Their coat of arms is simply a lichen. I saw it painted on the pines and oaks. Their attics were in the tops of the trees. They are of no politics. There was no noise of labour. I did not perceive that they were weaving or spinning. Yet I did detect, when the wind lulled and hearing was done away, the finest imaginable sweet musical hum,—as of a distant hive in May, which perchance was the sound of their thinking. They had no idle thoughts, and no one without could see their work, for their industry was not as in knots and excrescences embayed.

But I find it difficult to remember them. They fade irrevocably out of my mind even now while I speak and endeavour to recall them, and recollect myself. It is only after a long and serious effort to recollect my best thoughts that I become again aware of their cohabitancy. If it were not for such families as this, I think I should move out of Concord.

We are accustomed to say in New England that few and fewer pigeons visit us every year. Our forests furnish no mast for them. So, it would seem, few and fewer thoughts visit each growing man from year to year, for the grove in our minds is laid waste,—sold feed unnecessary fires of ambition, or sent to mill, and there is scarcely a twig left for them to perch on. They no longer build nor breed with us. In some more genial season, perchance, a faint shadow flits across the landscape of the mind, cast by the *wings* of some thought in its vernal or autumnal migration, but, looking up, we are unable to detect the substance of the thought itself. Our winged thoughts are turned to poultry. They no longer soar, and they attain only to a Shanghai and Cochin-China grandeur. Those *gra-a-ate thoughts*, those *gra-a-ate men* you hear of!

We hug the earth—how rarely we mount! Methinks we might elevate ourselves a little more. We might climb a tree, at least. I found my account in climbing a tree once. It was a tall white pine, on the top of a hill; and though I got well pitched, I was well paid for it, for I discovered new mountains in the horizon which I had never seen before,—so much more of the earth and the heavens. I might have walked about the foot of the tree for threescore years and ten, and yet I certainly should never have seen them. But, above all, I discovered around me,—it was near the end of June,—on the ends of the topmost branches only, a few minute and delicate red cone-like blossoms, the fertile flower of the white pine looking heavenward. I carried straightway to the village the topmost spire, and showed it to stranger jurymen who walked the streets,—for it was court-week,—and to farmers and lumber-dealers and wood-choppers and hunters, and not one had ever seen the like before, but they wondered as at a star dropped down. Tell of ancient architects finishing their works on the tops of columns as perfectly as on the lower and more visible parts! Nature has from the first expanded the minute blossoms of the forest only toward the heavens, above men's heads and unobserved by them. We see only the flowers that are under our feet in the meadows. The pines have developed their delicate blossoms on the highest twigs of the wood every summer for ages, as well over the heads of Nature's red children as of her white ones; yet scarcely a farmer or hunter in the land has ever seen them.

Above all, we cannot afford not to live in the present. He is blessed over all mortals who loses no moment of the passing life in remembering the past. Unless our philosophy hears the cock crow in every barn-yard within our horizon, it is belated. That sound commonly reminds us that we are growing rusty and antique in our employments and habits of thought. His philosophy comes down to a more recent time than ours. There is something suggested by it that is a newer testament—the gospel according to this moment. He has not fallen astern; he has got up early and kept up early, and to be where he is to be in season, in the foremost rank of time. It is an expression of the health and soundness of Nature, a brag for all the world,—healthiness as of a spring burst forth, a new fountain of the Muses, to celebrate this last instant of time. Where he lives no fugitive slave laws are passed. Who has not betrayed his master many times since last he heard the note?

The merit of this bird's strain is in its freedom from all plaintiveness. The singer can easily move us to tears or to laughter, but where is he who can excite in us a pure morning joy? When, in doleful dumps, breaking the awful stillness of our wooden sidewalk on a Sunday, or, perchance, a watcher in the house of mourning, I hear a cockerel crow far or near, I think to myself, "There is one of us well, at any rate,"—and with a sudden gush return to my senses.

We had a remarkable sunset one day last November. I was walking in a meadow, the source of a small brook, when the sun at last, just before setting, after a cold grey day, reached a clear stratum in the horizon, and the softest, brightest morning sunlight fell on the dry grass and on the stems of the trees in the opposite horizon, and on the leaves of the shrub-oaks on the hillside, while our shadows stretched long over the meadow eastward, as if we were the only motes in its beams. It was such a light as we could not have imagined a moment before, and the air also was so warm and serene that nothing was wanting to make a paradise of that meadow. When we reflected that this was not a solitary phenomenon, never to happen again, but that it would happen for ever and ever an infinite number of evenings, and cheer and reassure the latest child that walked there, it was more glorious still.

The sun sets on some retired meadow, where no house is visible, with all the glory and splendour that it lavishes on cities, and, perchance, as it has never set before,—where there is but a solitary marsh-hawk to have his wings gilded by it, or only a musquash looks out from his cabin, and there is some little black-veined brook in the midst of the marsh, just beginning to meander, winding slowly round a decaying stump. We walked in so pure and bright a light, gilding the withered grass and leaves, so softly and serenely bright, I thought I had never bathed in such a golden flood, without a ripple or a murmur to it. The west side of every wood and rising ground gleamed like the boundary of Elysium, and the sun on our backs seemed like a gentle herdsman driving us home at evening.

So we saunter toward the Holy Land, till one day the sun shall shine more brightly than ever he has done, shall perchance shine into our minds and hearts, and light up our whole lives with a great awakening light, as warm and serene and golden as on a bank-side in autumn.

H. D. Thoreau.

A Young Tramp

A plan had occurred to me for passing the night, which I was going to carry into execution. This was, to lie behind the wall at the back of my old school, in a corner where there used to be a haystack. I imagined it would be a kind of company to have the boys, and the bedroom where I used to tell the stories, so near me: although the boys would know nothing of my being there, and the bedroom would yield me no shelter.

I had had a hard day's work, and was pretty well jaded when I came climbing out, at last, upon the level of Blackheath. It cost me some trouble to find out Salem House; but I found it, and I found a haystack in the corner, and I lay down by it; having first walked round the wall, and looked up at the windows, and seen that all was dark and silent within. Never shall I forget the lonely sensation of first lying down, without a roof above my head.

Sleep came upon me as it came on many other outcasts, against whom house-doors were locked, and house-dogs barked, that night—and I dreamed of lying on my old school-bed, talking to the boys in my room; and found myself sitting upright, with Steerforth's name upon my lips, looking wildly at the stars that were glistening and glimmering above me. When I remembered where I was at that untimely hour, a feeling stole upon me that made me get up, afraid of I don't know what, and walk about. But the faint glimmering of the stars, and the pale light in the sky where the day was coming, reassured me: and my eyes being very heavy, I lay down again, and slept—though with a knowledge in my sleep that it was cold—until the warm beams of the sun, and the ringing of the getting-up bell at Salem House, awoke me. If I could have hoped that Steerforth was there, I would have lurked about until he came out alone; but I knew he must have left long since. Traddles still remained, perhaps, but it was very doubtful; and I had not sufficient confidence in his discretion or good luck, however strong my reliance was on his good-nature, to wish to trust him with my situation. So I crept away from the wall as Mr Creakle's boys were getting up, and struck into the long dusty track which I had first known to be the Dover Road when I was one of them, and when I little expected that any eyes would ever see me the wayfarer I was now, upon it.

What a different Sunday morning from the old Sunday morning at Yarmouth! In due time I heard the church-bells ringing, as I plodded on; and I met people who were going to church; and I passed a church or two where the congregation were inside, and the sound of singing came out into the sunshine, while the beadle sat and cooled himself in the shade of the porch, or stood beneath the yew-tree, with his hand to his forehead, glowering at me going by. But the peace and rest of the old Sunday morning were on everything, except me. That was the difference. I felt quite wicked in my dirt and dust, with my tangled hair. But for the quiet picture I had conjured up, of my mother in her youth and beauty, weeping by the fire, and my aunt relenting to her, I hardly think I should have had courage to go on until next day. But it always went before me, and I followed.

I got, that Sunday, through three-and-twenty miles on the straight road, though not very easily, for I was new to that kind of toil. I see myself, as evening closes in, coming over the bridge at Rochester, footsore and tired, and eating bread that I had bought for supper. One or two little houses, with the notice, "Lodgings for Travellers," hanging out, had tempted me; but I was afraid of spending the few pence I had, and was even more afraid of the vicious looks of the trampers I had met or overtaken. I sought no shelter, therefore, but the sky; and toiling into Chatham,—which, in that night's aspect, is a mere dream of chalk, and drawbridges, and mastless ships in a muddy river, roofed like Noah's arks,—crept, at last, upon a sort of grass-grown battery overhanging a lane, where a sentry was walking to and fro. Here I lay down, near a cannon; and, happy in the society of the sentry's footsteps, though he knew no more of my being above him than the boys at Salem House had known of my lying by the wall, slept soundly until morning.

Charles Dickens,—"David Copperfield."

"BETTER THAN THE GIG!"

Mr Pecksniff's horse being regarded in the light of a sacred animal, only to be driven by him, the chief priest of that temple, or by some person distinctly nominated for the time being to that high office by himself, the two young men agreed to walk to Salisbury; and so, when the time came, they set off on foot; which was, after all, a better mode of travelling than in the gig, as the weather was very cold and very dry.

Better! A rare strong, hearty, healthy walk—four statute miles an hour—preferable to that rumbling, tumbling, jolting, shaking, scraping, creaking, villainous old gig? Why, the two things will not admit of comparison. It is an insult to the walk, to set them side by side. Where is an instance of a gig having ever circulated a man's blood, unless when, putting him in danger of his neck, it awakened in his veins and in his ears, and all along his spine, a tingling heat, much more peculiar than agreeable? When did a gig ever sharpen anybody's wits and energies, unless it was when the horse bolted, and, crashing madly down a steep hill with a stone wall at the bottom, his desperate circumstances suggested to the only gentleman left inside, some novel and unheard-of mode of dropping out behind? Better than the gig!

The air was cold, Tom; so it was, there was no denying it; but would it have been more genial in the gig? The blacksmith's fire burned very bright, and leaped up high, as though it wanted men to warm; but would it have been less tempting, looked at from the clammy cushions of a gig? The wind blew keenly, nipping the features of the hardy wight who fought his way along; blinding him with his own hair if he had enough of it, and wintry dust if he hadn't; stopped his breath as though he had been soused in a cold bath; tearing aside his wrappings-up, and whistling in the very marrow of his bones; but it would have done all this a hundred times more fiercely to a man in a gig, wouldn't it? A fig for gigs!

Better than the gig! When were travellers by wheels and hoofs seen with such red-hot cheeks as those? when were they so good-humouredly and merrily bloused? when did their laughter ring upon the air, as they turned them round, what time the stronger gusts came sweeping up; and, facing round again as they passed by, dashed on, in such a glow of ruddy health as nothing could keep pace with, but the high spirits it engendered? Better than the gig! Why, here *is* a man in a gig coming the same way now. Look at him as he passes his whip into his left hand, chafes his numbed right fingers on his granite leg, and beats those marble toes of his upon the footboard. Ha, ha, ha! Who would exchange this rapid hurry of the blood for yonder stagnant misery, though its pace were twenty miles for one?

Better than the gig! No man in a gig could have such interest in the milestones. No man in a gig could see, or feel, or think, like merry users of their legs. How, as the wind sweeps on, upon these breezy downs, it tracks its flight in darkening ripples on the grass, and smoothest shadows on the hills! Look round and round upon this bare black plain, and see even here, upon a winter's day, how beautiful the shadows are! Alas! it is the nature of their kind to be so. The loveliest things in life, Tom, are but shadows; and they come and go, and change and fade away, as rapidly as these!

Another mile, and then begins a fall of snow, making the crow, who skims away so close above the ground to shirk the wind, a blot of ink upon the landscape. But though it drives and drifts against them as they walk, stiffening on their skirts, and freezing in the lashes of their eyes, they wouldn't have it fall more sparingly, no, not so much as by a single flake, although they had to go a score of miles. And, lo! the towers of the Old Cathedral rise before them, even now! and by-and-bye they come into the sheltered streets, made strangely silent by their white carpet; and so to the Inn for which they are bound; where they present such flushed and burning faces to the cold waiter, and are so brimful of vigour, that he almost feels assaulted by their presence; and, having nothing to oppose to the attack (being fresh, or rather stale, from the blazing fire in the coffee-room), is quite put out of his pale countenance.

Charles Dickens,—"Martin Chuzzlewit."

De Quincey leads the Simple Life

There were already, even in those days of 1802, numerous inns, erected at reasonable distances from each other, for the accommodation of tourists: and no sort of disgrace attached in Wales, as too generally upon the great roads of England, to the pedestrian style of travelling. Indeed, the majority of those whom I met as fellow-tourists in the quiet little cottage-parlours of the Welsh posting-houses were pedestrian travellers. All the way from Shrewsbury through Llangollen, Llanrwst, Conway, Bangor, then turning to the left at right angles through Carnarvon, and so on to Dolgelly (the chief town of Merionethshire), Tan-y-Bwlch, Harlech, Barmouth, and through the sweet solitudes of Cardiganshire, or turning back sharply towards the English border through the gorgeous wood scenery of Montgomeryshire—everywhere at intermitting distances of twelve to sixteen miles, I found the most comfortable inns. One feature indeed of repose in all this chain of solitary resting-houses—viz., the fact that none of them rose above two storeys in height—was due to the modest scale on which the travelling system of the Principality had moulded itself in correspondence to the calls of England, which then (but be it remembered this *then* was in 1802, a year of peace) threw a very small proportion of her vast migratory population annually into this sequestered channel. No huge Babylonian centres of commerce towered into the clouds on these sweet sylvan routes: no hurricanes of haste, or fever-stricken armies of horses and flying chariots, tormented the echoes in these mountain recesses. And it has often struck me that a world-wearied man, who sought for the peace of monasteries separated from their gloomy captivity—peace and silence such as theirs combined with the large liberty of nature— could not do better than revolve amongst these modest inns in the five northern Welsh counties of Denbigh, Montgomery, Carnarvon, Merioneth, and Cardigan. Sleeping, for instance, and breakfasting at Carnarvon; then, by an easy nine-mile walk, going forwards to dinner at Bangor, thence to Aber—nine miles; or to Llanberris; and so on for ever, accomplishing seventy to ninety or one hundred miles in a week. This, upon actual experiment, and for week after week, I found the most delightful of lives. Here was the eternal motion of winds and rivers, or of the Wandering Jew liberated from the persecution which compelled him to move, and turned his breezy freedom into a killing captivity. Happier life I cannot imagine than this vagrancy, if the weather were but tolerable, through endless successions of changing beauty, and towards evening a courteous welcome in a pretty rustic home—that having all the luxuries of a fine hotel (in particular some luxuries [1] that are almost sacred to Alpine regions), was at the same time liberated from the inevitable accompaniments of such hotels in great cities or at great travelling stations—viz., the tumult and uproar.

Life on this model was but too delightful; and to myself especially, that am never thoroughly in health unless when having pedestrian exercise to the extent of fifteen miles at the most, and eight to ten miles at the least. Living thus, a man earned his daily enjoyment. But what did it cost? About half a guinea a day: whilst my boyish allowance was not a third of this. The flagrant health, health boiling over in fiery rapture, which ran along, side by side, with exercise on this scale, whilst all the while from morning to night I was inhaling mountain air, soon passed into a hateful scourge. Perquisites to servants and a bed would have absorbed the whole of my weekly guinea. My policy therefore was, if the autumnal air was warm enough, to save this expense of a bed and the chambermaid by sleeping amongst ferns or furze upon a hillside; and perhaps with a cloak of sufficient *weight* as well as compass, or an Arab's burnoose, this would have been no great hardship. But then in the daytime what an oppressive burden to carry! So perhaps it was as well that I had no cloak at all. I did, however, for some weeks try the plan of carrying a canvas tent manufactured by myself, and not larger than an ordinary umbrella: but to pitch this securely I found difficult; and on windy nights it became a troublesome companion. As winter drew near, this bivouacking system became too dangerous to attempt. Still one may bivouack decently, barring rain and wind, up to the end of October. And I counted, on the whole, that in a fortnight I spent nine nights abroad. There are, as perhaps the reader knows by experience, no jaguars in Wales—nor pumas—nor anacondas—nor (generally speaking) any Thugs. What I feared most, but perhaps only through ignorance of zoology, was, lest, whilst my sleeping face was upturned to the stars, some one of the many little Brahminical-looking cows on the Cambrian hills, one or other, might poach her foot into the centre of my face. I do not suppose any fixed hostility of that nature to English faces in Welsh

---

[1] But a luxury of another class, and quite peculiar to Wales, was in those days (I hope in these) the Welsh harp, in attendance at every inn.

cows: but everywhere I observe in the feminine mind something of beautiful caprice, a floral exuberance of that charming wilfulness which characterises our dear human sisters I fear through all worlds. Against Thugs I had Juvenal's license to be careless in the emptiness of my pockets (*cantabit vacuus coram latrone viator*). But I fear that Juvenal's license will not always hold water. There are people bent upon cudgelling one who will persist in excusing one's having nothing but a bad shilling in one's purse, without reading in that Juvenalian *vacuitas* any privilege or license of exemption from the general fate of travellers that intrude upon the solitude of robbers.

Thomas de Quincey.

A Resolution

I had long ago determined to leave London as soon as the means should be in my power, and, now that they were, I determined to leave the Great City; yet I felt some reluctance to go. I would fain have pursued the career of original authorship which had just opened itself to me, and have written other tales of adventure. The bookseller had given me encouragement enough to do so; he had assured me that he should be always happy to deal with me for an article (that was the word) similar to the one I had brought him, provided my terms were moderate; and the bookseller's wife, by her complimentary language, had given me yet more encouragement. But for some months past I had been far from well, and my original indisposition, brought on partly by the peculiar atmosphere of the Big City, partly by anxiety of mind, had been much increased by the exertions which I had been compelled to make during the last few days. I felt that, were I to remain where I was, I should die, or become a confirmed valetudinarian. I would go forth into the country, travelling on foot, and, by exercise and inhaling pure air, endeavour to recover my health, leaving my subsequent movements to be determined by Providence.

But whither should I bend my course? Once or twice I thought of walking home to the old town, stay some time with my mother and my brother, and enjoy the pleasant walks in the neighbourhood; but, though I wished very much to see my mother and my brother, and felt much disposed to enjoy the said pleasant walks, the old town was not exactly the place to which I wished to go at this present juncture. I was afraid the people would ask, Where are your Northern Ballads? Where are your alliterative translations from Ab Gwilym—of which you were always talking, and with which you promised to astonish the world? Now, in the event of such interrogations, what could I answer? It is true I had compiled Newgate Lives and Trials, and had written the life of Joseph Sell, but I was afraid that the people of the old town would scarcely consider these as equivalents for the Northern Ballads and the songs of Ab Gwilym. I would go forth and wander in any direction but that of the old town.

But how one's sensibility on any particular point diminishes with time; at present, I enter the old town perfectly indifferent as to what the people may be thinking on the subject of the songs and ballads. With respect to the people themselves, whether, like my sensibility, their curiosity has altogether evaporated, or whether, which is at least equally probable, they never entertained any, one thing is certain, that never in a single instance have they troubled me with any remarks on the subject of the songs and ballads.

As it was my intention to travel on foot, with a bundle and a stick, I despatched my trunk containing some few clothes and books to the old town. My preparations were soon made; in about three days I was in readiness to start.

STONEHENGE

After standing still a minute or two, considering what I should do, I moved down what appeared to be the street of a small straggling town; presently I passed by a church, which rose indistinctly on my right hand; anon there was the rustling of foliage and the rushing of waters. I reached a bridge, beneath which a small stream was running in the direction of the south. I stopped and leaned over the parapet, for I have always loved to look upon streams, especially at the still hours. "What stream is this, I wonder?" said I, as I looked down from the parapet into the water, which whirled and gurgled below.

Leaving the bridge, I ascended a gentle acclivity, and presently reached what appeared to be a tract of moory undulating ground. It was now tolerably light, but there was a mist or haze abroad which prevented my seeing objects with much precision. I felt chill in the damp air of the early morn, and walked rapidly forward. In about half an hour I arrived where the road divided into two, at an angle or tongue of dark green sward. "To the right or the left?" said I, and forthwith took, without knowing why, the left-hand road, along which I proceeded about a hundred yards, when, in the midst of the tongue of sward formed by the two roads, collaterally with myself, I perceived what I at first conceived to be a small grove of blighted trunks of oaks, barked and grey. I stood still for a moment, and then, turning off the road, advanced slowly towards it over the sward; as I drew nearer, I perceived that the objects which had attracted my curiosity, and which formed a kind of circle, were not trees, but immense upright stones. A thrill pervaded my system; just before me were two, the mightiest of the whole, tall as the stems of proud oaks, supporting on their tops a huge transverse stone, and forming a wonderful doorway. I knew now where I was, and, laying down my stick and bundle, and taking off my hat, I advanced slowly, and cast myself—it was folly, perhaps, but I could not help what I did—cast myself, with my face on the dewy earth, in the middle of the portal of giants, beneath the transverse stone.

The spirit of Stonehenge was strong upon me!

And after I had remained with my face on the ground for some time, I arose, placed my hat on my head, and, taking up my stick and bundle, wandered around the wondrous circle, examining each individual stone, from the greatest to the least; and then, entering by the great door, seated myself upon an immense broad stone, one side of which was supported by several small ones, and the other slanted upon the earth; and there in deep meditation, I sat for an hour or two, till the sun shone in my face above the tall stones of the eastern side.

And as I still sat there, I heard the noise of bells, and presently a large number of sheep came browsing past the circle of stones; two or three entered, and grazed upon what they could find, and soon a man also entered the circle at the northern side.

"Early here, sir," said the man, who was tall, and dressed in a dark green slop, and had all the appearance of a shepherd; "a traveller, I suppose?"

"Yes," said I, "I am a traveller; are these sheep yours?"

"They are, sir; that is, they are my master's. A strange place this, sir," said he, looking at the stones; "ever here before?"

"Never in body, frequently in mind."

"Heard of the stones, I suppose; no wonder—all the people of the plain talk of them."

"What do the people of the plain say of them?"

"Why, they say—How did they ever come here?"

"Do they not suppose them to have been brought?"

"Who should have brought them?"

"I have read that they were brought by many thousand men."

"Where from?"

"Ireland."

"How did they bring them?"

"I don't know."

"And what did they bring them for?"

"To form a temple, perhaps."

"What is that?"

"A place to worship God in."

"A strange place to worship God in."

"Why?"

"It has no roof."

"Yes, it has."

"Where?" said the man, looking up.

"What do you see above you?"

"The sky."

"Well?"

"Well!"

"Have you anything to say?"

"How did those stones come here?"

"Are there other stones like these on the plains?" said I.

"None; and yet there are plenty of strange things on these downs."

"What are they?"

"Strange heaps, and barrows, and great walls of earth built on the top of hills."

"Do the people of the plain wonder how they came there?"

"They do not."

"Why?"

"They were raised by hands."

"And these stones?"

"How did they ever come here?"

"I wonder whether they are here?" said I.

"These stones?"

"Yes."

"So sure as the world," said the man; "and as the world, they will stand as long."

"I wonder whether there is a world."

"What do you mean?"

"An earth and sea, moon and stars, sheep and men."

"Do you doubt it?"

"Sometimes."

"I never heard it doubted before."

"It is impossible there should be a world."

"It ain't possible there shouldn't be a world."

"Just so." At this moment a fine ewe, attended by a lamb, rushed into the circle and fondled the knees of the shepherd. "I suppose you would not care to have some milk?" said the man.

"Why do you suppose so?"

"Because, so be, there be no sheep, no milk, you know; and what there ben't is not worth having."

"You could not have argued better," said I, "that is, supposing you have argued; with respect to the milk you may do as you please."

"Be still, Nanny," said the man; and producing a tin vessel from his scrip, he milked the ewe into it. "Here is milk of the plains, master," said the man, as he handed the vessel to me.

"Where are those barrows and great walls of earth you were speaking of?" said I, after I had drunk some of the milk; "are there any near where we are?"

"Not within many miles; the nearest is yonder away," said the shepherd, pointing to the south-east. "It's a grand place, that, but not like this; quite different, and from it you have a sight of the finest spire in the world."

"I must go to it," said I, and I drank the remainder of the milk; "yonder, you say."

"Yes, yonder; but you cannot get to it in that direction, the river lies between."

"What river?"

"The Avon."

"Avon is British," said I.

"Yes," said the man, "we are all British here."

"No, we are not," said I.

"What are we, then?"

"English."

"A'n't they one?"

"No."

"Who were the British?"

"The men who are supposed to have worshipped God in this place, and who raised these stones."

"Where are they now?"

"Our forefathers slaughtered them, spilled their blood all about, especially in this neighbourhood, destroyed their pleasant places, and left not, to use their own words, one stone upon another."

"Yes, they did," said the shepherd, looking aloft at the transverse stone.

"And it is well for them they did; whenever that stone, which English hands never raised, is by English hands thrown down, woe, woe, woe to the English race; spare it, English! Hengist spared it!— Here is sixpence."

"I won't have it," said the man.

"Why not?"

"You talk so prettily about these stones; you seem to know all about them."

"I never receive presents; with respect to the stones, I say with yourself, How did they ever come here?"

"How did they ever come here?" said the shepherd.

A PROSPECT

Leaving the shepherd, I bent my way in the direction pointed out by him as that in which the most remarkable of the strange remains of which he had spoken lay. I proceeded rapidly, making my way over the downs covered with coarse grass and fern; with respect to the river of which he had spoken, I reflected that, either by wading or swimming, I could easily transfer myself and what I bore to the opposite side. On arriving at its banks, I found it a beautiful stream, but shallow, with here and there a deep place, where the water ran dark and still.

Always fond of the pure lymph, I undressed, and plunged into one of these gulfs, from which I emerged, my whole frame in a glow, and tingling with delicious sensations. After conveying my clothes and scanty baggage to the farther side, I dressed, and then with hurried steps bent my course in the direction of some lofty ground; I at length found myself on a high road, leading over wide and arid downs; following the road for some miles without seeing anything remarkable, I supposed at length that I had taken the wrong path, and wended on slowly and disconsolately for some time, till, having nearly surmounted a steep hill, I knew at once, from certain appearances, that I was near the object of my search. Turning to the right near the brow of the hill, I proceeded along a path which brought me to a causeway leading over a deep ravine, and connecting the hill with another which had once formed part of it, for the ravine was evidently the work of art. I passed over the causeway, and found myself in a kind of gateway which admitted me into a square space of many acres, surrounded on all sides by mounds or ramparts of earth. Though I had never been in such a place before, I knew that I stood within the precincts of what had been a Roman encampment, and one probably of the largest size, for many thousand warriors might have found room to perform their evolutions in that space, in which corn was now growing, the green ears waving in the morning wind.

After I had gazed about the space for a time, standing in the gateway formed by the mounds, I clambered up the mound to the left hand, and on the top of that mound I found myself at a great altitude; beneath, at the distance of a mile, was a fair old city, situated amongst verdant meadows, watered with streams, and from the heart of that old city, from amidst mighty trees, I beheld towering to the sky the finest spire in the world.

After I had looked from the Roman rampart for a long time, I hurried away, and, retracing my steps along the causeway, regained the road, and, passing over the brow of the hill, descended to the city of the spire.

"ONE OF THE PLEASANT MOMENTS OF LIFE"

After walking about a dozen miles, I came to a town, where I rested for the night. The next morning I set out again in the direction of the north-west. I continued journeying for four days, my daily journeys varying from twenty to twenty-five miles. During this time nothing occurred to me worthy of any especial notice. The weather was brilliant, and I rapidly improved both in strength and spirits. On the fifth day, about two o'clock, I arrived at a small town. Feeling hungry, I entered a decent-looking inn—within a kind of bar I saw a huge, fat, landlord-looking person, with a very pretty, smartly-dressed maiden. Addressing myself to the fat man, "House!" said I, "house! Can I have dinner, house?" "Young gentleman," said the huge fat landlord, "you are come at the right time; dinner will be taken up in a few minutes, and such a dinner," he continued, rubbing his hands, "as you will not see every day in these times."

"I am hot and dusty," said I, "and should wish to cool my hands and face."

"Jenny!" said the huge landlord, with the utmost gravity, "show the gentleman into number seven, that he may wash his hands and face."

"By no means," said I, "I am a person of primitive habits, and there is nothing like the pump in weather like this."

"Jenny!" said the landlord, with the same gravity as before, "go with the young gentleman to the pump in the back kitchen, and take a clean towel along with you."

Thereupon the rosy-faced clean-looking damsel went to a drawer, and producing a large, thick, but snowy-white towel, she nodded to me to follow her; whereupon I followed Jenny through a long passage into the back kitchen.

And at the end of the back kitchen there stood a pump; and going to it I placed my hands beneath the spout, and said, "Pump, Jenny"; and Jenny incontinently, without laying down the towel, pumped with one hand, and I washed and cooled my heated hands.

And, when my hands were washed and cooled, I took off my neckcloth, and unbuttoning my shirt collar, I placed my head beneath the spout of the pump, and I said unto Jenny, "Now, Jenny, lay down the towel, and pump for your life."

Thereupon Jenny, placing the towel on a linen-horse, took the handle of the pump with both hands and pumped over my head as handmaid had never pumped before; so that the water poured in torrents from my head, my face, and my hair down upon the brick floor.

And after the lapse of somewhat more than a minute, I called out with a half-strangled voice, "Hold, Jenny!" and Jenny desisted. I stood for a few moments to recover my breath, then taking the towel which Jenny proffered, I dried composedly my hands and head, my face and hair; then, returning the towel to Jenny, I gave a deep sigh and said, "Surely this is one of the pleasant moments of life."

George Borrow,—"Lavengro."

The Snowdon Ranger

I quickened my steps, and soon came up to the two individuals. One was an elderly man, dressed in a smock frock, and with a hairy cap on his head. The other was much younger, wore a hat, and was dressed in a coarse suit of blue, nearly new, and doubtless his Sunday's best. He was smoking a pipe. I greeted them in English, and sat down near them. They responded in the same language, the younger man with considerable civility and briskness, the other in a tone of voice denoting some reserve.

"May I ask the name of this lake?" said I, addressing myself to the young man, who sat between me and the elderly one.

"Its name is Llyn Cwellyn, sir," said he, taking the pipe out of his mouth. "And a fine lake it is."

"Plenty of fish in it?" I demanded.

"Plenty, sir; plenty of trout and pike and char."

"Is it deep?" said I.

"Near the shore it is shallow, sir, but in the middle and near the other side it is deep, so deep that no one knows how deep it is."

"What is the name," said I, "of the great black mountain there on the other side?"

"It is called Mynydd Mawr, or the Great Mountain. Yonder rock, which bulks out from it, down the lake yonder, and which you passed as you came along, is called Castell Cidwm, which means Wolf's rock or castle."

"Did a wolf ever live there?" I demanded.

"Perhaps so," said the man, "for I have heard say that there were wolves of old in Wales."

"And what is the name of the beautiful hill yonder, before us across the water?"

"That, sir, is called Cairn Drws y Coed," said the man.

"The stone heap of the gate of the wood," said I.

"Are you Welsh, sir?" said the man.

"No," said I, "but I know something of the language of Wales. I suppose you live in that house?"

"Not exactly, sir; my father-in-law here lives in that house, and my wife with him. I am a miner, and spend six days in the week at my mine, but every Sunday I come here, and pass the day with my wife and him."

"And what profession does he follow?" said I; "is he a fisherman?"

"Fisherman!" said the elderly man contemptuously, "not I. I am the Snowdon Ranger."

"And what is that?" said I.

The elderly man tossed his head proudly, and made no reply.

"A ranger means a guide, sir," said the younger man—"my father-in-law is generally termed the Snowdon Ranger because he is a tip-top guide, and he has named the house after him the Snowdon Ranger. He entertains gentlemen in it who put themselves under his guidance in order to ascend Snowdon and to see the country."

"There is some difference in your professions," said I; "he deals in heights, you in depths; both, however, are break-necky trades."

"I run more risk from gunpowder than anything else," said the younger man. "I am a slate-miner, and am continually blasting. I have, however, had my falls. Are you going far to-night, sir?"

"I am going to Bethgelert," said I.

"A good six miles, sir, from here. Do you come from Caernarvon?"

"Farther than that," said I. "I come from Bangor."

"To-day, sir, and walking?"

"To-day, and walking."

"You must be rather tired, sir; you came along the valley very slowly."

"I am not in the slightest degree tired," said I; "when I start from here, I shall put on my best pace, and soon get to Bethgelert."

"Anybody can get along over level ground," said the old man, laconically.

"Not with equal swiftness," said I. "I do assure you, friend, to be able to move at a good swinging pace over level ground is something not to be sneezed at. Not," said I, lifting up my voice, "that I would for a moment compare walking on the level ground to mountain ranging, pacing along the road to springing up crags like a mountain goat, or assert that even Powell himself, the first of all road walkers, was entitled to so bright a wreath of fame as the Snowdon Ranger."

"Won't you walk in, sir?" said the elderly man.

"No, I thank you," said I; "I prefer sitting out here, gazing on the lake and the noble mountains."

"I wish you would, sir," said the elderly man, "and take a glass of something; I will charge you nothing."

"Thank you," said I—"I am in want of nothing, and shall presently start. Do many people ascend Snowdon from your house?"

"Not so many as I could wish," said the ranger; "people in general prefer ascending Snowdon from that trumpery place Bethgelert; but those who do are fools—begging your honour's pardon. The place to ascend Snowdon from is my house. The way from my house up Snowdon is wonderful for the romantic scenery which it affords; that from Bethgelert can't be named in the same day with it for scenery; moreover, from my house you may have the best guide in Wales; whereas the guides of Bethgelert—but I say nothing. If your honour is bound for the Wyddfa, as I suppose you are, you had better start from my house to-morrow under my guidance."

"I have already been up the Wyddfa from Llanberis," said I, "and am now going through Bethgelert to Llangollen, where my family are; were I going up Snowdon again, I should most certainly start from your house under your guidance, and were I not in a hurry at present, I would certainly take up my quarters here for a week, and every day make excursions with you into the recesses of Eryri. I suppose you are acquainted with all the secrets of the hills?"

"Trust the old ranger for that, your honour. I would show your honour the black lake in the frightful hollow, in which the fishes have monstrous heads and little bodies, the lake on which neither swan, duck nor any kind of wildfowl was ever seen to light. Then I would show your honour the fountain of the hopping creatures, where, where——"

"Were you ever at that Wolf's crag, that Castell y Cidwm?" said I.

"Can't say I ever was, your honour. You see it lies so close by, just across that lake, that——"

"You thought you could see it any day, and so never went," said I. "Can't you tell me whether there are any ruins upon it?"

"I can't, your honour."

"I shouldn't wonder," said I, "if in old times it was the stronghold of some robber-chieftain; cidwm in the old Welsh is frequently applied to a ferocious man. Castell Cidwm, I should think, rather ought to be translated the robber's castle, than the wolf's rock. If I ever come into these parts again, you and I will visit it together, and see what kind of a place it is. Now farewell! It is getting late." I then departed.

"What a nice gentleman!" said the younger man, when I was a few yards distant.

"I never saw a nicer gentleman," said the old ranger.

I sped along, Snowdon on my left, the lake on my right, and the tip of a mountain peak right before me in the east. After a little time I looked back; what a scene! The silver lake and the shadowy mountain over its southern side looking now, methought, very much like Gibraltar. I lingered and lingered, gazing and gazing, and at last only by an effort tore myself away. The evening had now become delightfully cool in this land of wonders. On I sped, passing by two noisy brooks coming from Snowdon to pay tribute to the lake. And now I had left the lake and the valley behind, and was ascending a hill. As I gained its summit, up rose the moon to cheer my way. In a little time, a wild stony gorge confronted me, a stream ran down the gorge with hollow roar, a bridge lay across it. I asked a figure whom I saw standing by the bridge the place's name. "Rhyd du"—the black ford—I crossed the bridge. The voice of the Methodist was yelling from a little chapel on my left. I went to the door and listened: "When the sinner takes hold of God, God takes hold of the sinner." The voice was frightfully hoarse. I passed on;

night fell fast around me, and the mountain to the south-east, towards which I was tending, looked blackly grand. And now I came to a milestone, on which I read with difficulty: "Three miles to Bethgelert." The way for some time had been upward, but now it was downward. I reached a torrent, which, coming from the north-west, rushed under a bridge, over which I passed. The torrent attended me on my right hand the whole way to Bethgelert. The descent now became very rapid. I passed a pine wood on my left, and proceeded for more than two miles at a tremendous rate. I then came to a wood—this wood was just above Bethgelert—proceeding in the direction of a black mountain, I found myself amongst houses, at the bottom of a valley. I passed over a bridge, and inquiring of some people, whom I met, the way to the inn, was shown an edifice brilliantly lighted up, which I entered.

OF UMBRELLAS

Wending my course to the north, I came to the white bare spot which I had seen from the moor, and which was in fact the top of a considerable elevation over which the road passed. Here I turned and looked at the hills I had come across. There they stood, darkly blue, a rain cloud, like ink, hanging over their summits. O, the wild hills of Wales, the land of old renown and of wonder, the land of Arthur and Merlin.

The road now lay nearly due west. Rain came on, but it was at my back, so I expanded my umbrella, flung it over my shoulder and laughed. O, how a man laughs who has a good umbrella when he has the rain at his back, aye and over his head too, and at all times when it rains except when the rain is in his face, when the umbrella is not of much service. O, what a good friend to a man is an umbrella in rain time, and likewise at many other times. What need he fear if a wild bull or a ferocious dog attacks him, provided he has a good umbrella? he unfurls the umbrella in the face of the bull or dog, and the brute turns round quite scared, and runs away. Or if a footpad asks him for his money, what need he care provided he has an umbrella? he threatens to dodge the ferrule into the ruffian's eye, and the fellow starts back and says, "Lord, sir! I meant no harm. I never saw you before in all my life. I merely meant a little fun." Moreover, who doubts that you are a respectable character provided you have an umbrella? you go into a public-house and call for a pot of beer, and the publican puts it down before you with one hand without holding out the other for the money, for he sees that you have an umbrella and consequently property. And what respectable man, when you overtake him on the way and speak to him, will refuse to hold conversation with you, provided you have an umbrella? No one. The respectable man sees you have an umbrella and concludes that you do not intend to rob him, and with justice, for robbers never carry umbrellas. O, a tent, a shield, a lance and a voucher for character is an umbrella. Amongst the very best friends of man must be reckoned an umbrella. [2]

The way lay over dreary, moory hills: at last it began to descend and I saw a valley below me with a narrow river running through it to which wooded hills sloped down; far to the west were blue mountains. The scene was beautiful but melancholy; the rain had passed away, but a gloomy almost November sky was above, and the mists of night were coming down apace.

I crossed a bridge at the bottom of the valley and presently saw a road branching to the right. I paused, but after a little time went straight forward. Gloomy woods were on each side of me and night had come down. Fear came upon me that I was not in the right road, but I saw no house at which I could inquire, nor did I see a single individual for miles of whom I could ask. At last I heard the sound of hatchets in a dingle on my right, and catching a glimpse of a gate at the head of a path, which led down into it, I got over it. After descending some time I hallooed. The noise of the hatchets ceased. I hallooed again, and a voice cried in Welsh, "What do you want?" "To know the way to Bala," I replied. There was no answer, but presently I heard steps, and the figure of a man drew nigh half undistinguishable in the darkness and saluted me. I returned his salutation, and told him I wanted to know the way to Bala. He told me, and I found I had been going right. I thanked him and regained the road. I sped onward and in about half an hour saw some houses, then a bridge, then a lake on my left, which I recognised as the lake of Bala. I skirted the end of it, and came to a street cheerfully lighted up, and in a minute more was in the White Lion Inn.

---

[2] As the umbrella is rather a hackneyed subject two or three things will of course be found in the above eulogium on an umbrella which have been said by other folks on that subject; the writer, however, flatters himself that in his eulogium on an umbrella two or three things will also be found which have never been said by any one else about an umbrella.

SUPPER—AND A MORNING VIEW

The sun was going down as I left the inn. I recrossed the streamlet by means of the pole and rail. The water was running with much less violence than in the morning, and was considerably lower. The evening was calm and beautifully cool, with a slight tendency to frost. I walked along with a bounding and elastic step, and never remember to have felt more happy and cheerful.

I reached the hospice at about six o'clock, a bright moon shining upon me, and found a capital supper awaiting me, which I enjoyed exceedingly.

How one enjoys one's supper at one's inn, after a good day's walk, provided one has the proud and glorious consciousness of being able to pay one's reckoning on the morrow!

The morning of the sixth was bright and glorious. As I looked from the window of the upper sitting-room of the hospice the scene which presented itself was wild and beautiful to a degree. The oak-covered tops of the volcanic crater were gilded with the brightest sunshine, whilst the eastern side remained in dark shade and the gap or narrow entrance to the north in shadow yet darker, in the midst of which shone the silver of the Rheidol cataract. Should I live a hundred years I shall never forget the wild fantastic beauty of that morning scene.

George Borrow,—"Wild Wales."

Song of the Open Road

Afoot and light-hearted I take to the open road!
Healthy, free, the world before me,
The long brown path before me, leading where-ever I choose!

Henceforth I ask not good-fortune, I myself am good-fortune,
Henceforth I whimper no more, postpone no more, need nothing,
Done with indoor complaints, libraries, querulous criticisms,
Strong and content I travel the open road.

The earth—that is sufficient,
I do not want the constellations any nearer,
I know they are very well where they are,
I know they suffice for those who belong to them.

Still here I carry my old delicious burdens,
I carry them, men and women—I carry them with me wherever I go,
I swear it is impossible for me to get rid of them,
I am fill'd with them, and I will fill them in return.

You road I travel and look around! I believe you are not all that is here!
I believe that something unseen is also here.

Here is the profound lesson of reception, neither preference or denial;
The black with his woolly head, the felon, the diseased, the illiterate person, are not denied,
The birth, the hasting after the physician, the beggar's tramp, the drunkard's stagger, the laughing party of mechanics,
The escaped youth, the rich person's carriage, the fop, the eloping couple,

The early market-man, the hearse, the moving of furniture into the town, the return back from the town,

They pass, I also pass, any thing passes, none can be interdicted,
None but are accepted, none but are dear to me.

You air that serves me with breath to speak!
You objects that call from diffusion my meanings and give them shape!
You light that wraps me and all things in delicate equable showers!
You paths worn in the irregular hollows by the road-sides!
I think you are latent with curious existences—you are so dear to me.

You flagg'd walks of the cities! you strong curbs at the edges!
You ferries! you planks and posts of wharves! you timber-lined sides! you distant ships!

You rows of houses! you window-pierced façades! you roofs!
You porches and entrances! you copings and iron guards!
You windows whose transparent shells might expose so much!
You doors and ascending steps! you arches!
You grey stones of interminable pavements! you trodden crossings!
From all that has been near you I believe you have imparted to yourselves, and now would impart the same secretly to me,
From the living and the dead I think you have peopled your impassive surfaces, and the spirits thereof would be evident and amicable with me.

The earth expanding right hand and left hand,
The picture alive, every part in its best light,
The music falling in where it is wanted, and stopping where it is not wanted,
The cheerful voice of the public road—the gay fresh sentiment of the road.

O highway I travel! O public road! Do you say to me, Do not leave me?
Do you say, Venture not?—If you leave me you are lost?
Do you say, I am already prepared—I am well beaten and undenied—adhere to me?

O public road! I say back I am not afraid to leave you—yet I love you,
You express me better than I can express myself,
You shall be more to me than my poem.

I think heroic deeds were all conceived in the open air,
I think I could stop here myself and do miracles,
I think whatever I meet on the road I shall like, and whoever beholds me shall like me,
I think whoever I see must be happy.

From this hour, freedom!
From this hour I ordain myself loosed of limits and imaginary lines!
Going where I list—my own master, total and absolute,
Listening to others, considering well what they say,
Pausing, searching, receiving, contemplating.
Gently but with undeniable will divesting myself of the holds that would hold me.
I inhale great draughts of air,
The east and the west are mine, and the north and the south are mine.

I am larger than I thought!
I did not know I held so much goodness!

All seems beautiful to me,
I can repeat over to men and women, You have done such good to me, I would do the same to you,
I will recruit for myself and you as I go,
I will scatter myself among men and women as I go,
I will toss a new gladness and roughness among them,
Whoever denies me it shall not trouble me,
Whoever accepts me he or she shall be blessed and shall bless me.

Now if a thousand perfect men were to appear, it would not amaze me,
Now if a thousand beautiful forms of women appear'd, it would not astonish me.

Now I see the secret of the making of the best persons,
It is to grow in the open air, and eat and sleep with the earth.

Here a great personal deed has room,
(Such a deed seizes upon the hearts of the whole race of men,
Its effusion of strength and will overwhelms laws and mocks all authority and all argument against it.)

Here is the test of wisdom,
Wisdom is not finally tested in schools,
Wisdom cannot be pass'd from one having it to another not having it,
Wisdom is of the soul, is not susceptible of proof, is its own proof,
Applies to all stages and objects and qualities and is content,
Is the certainty of the reality and immortality of things, and the excellence of things;
Something there is in the float of the sight of things that provokes it out of the soul.

Now I re-examine philosophies and religions,
They may prove well in lecture-rooms, yet not prove at all under the spacious clouds and along the landscape and flowing currents.

Here is realization,
Here is a man tallied—he realizes here what he has in him,
The past, the future, majesty, love—if they are vacant of you, you are vacant of them.

Only the kernel of every object nourishes;
Where is he who tears off the husks for you and me?
Where is he that undoes stratagems and envelopes for you and me?

Here is adhesiveness, it is not previously fashion'd, it is apropos;
Do you know what it is as you pass to be loved by strangers?
Do you know the talk of those turning eyeballs?

Here is the efflux of the soul,
The efflux of the soul comes from within through embower'd gates, ever provoking questions.
These yearnings why are they? these thoughts in the darkness why are they?

Why are there men and women that while they are nigh me the sunlight expands my blood?
Why when they leave me do my pennants of joy sink flat and lank?
Why are there trees I never walk under but large and melodious thoughts descend upon me?
(I think they hang there winter and summer on those trees and almost drop fruit as I pass;)
What is it I interchange so suddenly with strangers?
What with some driver as I ride on the seat by his side?
What with some fisherman drawing his seine by the shore as I walk by and pause?
What gives me to be free to a woman's and man's good-will? what gives them to be free to mine?

The efflux of the soul is happiness, here is happiness.
I think it pervades the open air, waiting at all times,
Now it flows unto us, we are rightly charged.

Here rises the fluid and attaching character,
The fluid and attaching character is the freshness and sweetness of man and woman,
(The herbs of the morning sprout no fresher and sweeter every day out of the roots of themselves, than it sprouts fresh and sweet continually out of itself.)

Toward the fluid and attaching character exudes the sweat of the love of young and old,
From it falls distill'd the charm that mocks beauty and attainments,
Toward it heaves the shuddering longing ache of contact.

Allons! whoever you are come travel with me.
Travelling with me you find what never tires.

The earth never tires,
The earth is rude, silent, incomprehensible at first, Nature is rude and incomprehensible at first,
Be not discouraged, keep on, there are divine things well envelop'd,
I swear to you there are divine things more beautiful than words can tell.

Allons! we must not stop here,

However sweet these laid-up stores, however convenient this dwelling we cannot remain here,
However shelter'd this port and however calm these waters we must not anchor here,
However welcome the hospitality that surrounds us we are permitted to receive it but a little while.

Allons! the inducements shall be greater,
We will sail pathless and wild seas,
We will go where winds blow, waves dash, and the Yankee clipper speeds by under full sail.

Allons! with power, liberty, the earth, the elements,
Health, defiance, gaiety, self-esteem, curiosity;
Allons! from all formulas!
From your formulas, O bat-eyed and materialistic priests.

The stale cadaver blocks up the passage—the burial waits no longer.

Allons! yet take warning!
He travelling with me needs the best blood, thews, endurance,
None may come to the trial till he or she bring courage and health,
Come not here if you have already spent the best of yourself,
Only those may come who come in sweet and determined bodies,
No diseas'd person, no rum drinker or venereal taint is permitted here.

(I and mine do not convince by arguments, similes, rhymes,
We convince by our presence.)

Listen! I will be honest with you,
I do not offer the old smooth prizes, but offer rough new prizes,
These are the days that must happen to you:
You shall not heap up what is call'd riches:
You shall scatter with lavish hand all that you earn or achieve,
You but arrive at the city to which you were destin'd, you hardly settle yourself to satisfaction before you are call'd by an irresistible call to depart,

You shall be treated to the ironical smiles and mockings of those who remain behind you,
What beckonings of love you receive you shall only answer with passionate kisses of parting,
You shall not allow the hold of those who spread their reach'd hands toward you.

Allons! after the great Companions, and to belong to them!
They too are on the road—they are the swift and majestic men—they are the greatest women,
Enjoyers of calms of seas and storms of seas,
Sailors of many a ship, walkers of many a mile of land,
Habitués of many distant countries, habitués of far distant dwellings,
Trusters of men and women, observers of cities, solitary toilers,
Pausers and contemplators of tufts, blossoms, shells of the shore,
Dancers at wedding-dances, kissers of brides, tender helpers of children, bearers of children,
Soldiers of revolts, standers by gaping graves, lowerers-down of coffins,
Journeyers over consecutive seasons, over the years, the curious years each emerging from that which preceded it,
Journeyers as with companions, namely their own diverse phases,
Forth-steppers from the latent unrealized baby-days,
Journeyers gaily with their own youth, journeyers with their bearded and well-grain'd manhood,
Journeyers with their womanhood, ample, unsurpass'd, content,
Journeyers with their own sublime old age, of manhood or womanhood,
Old age, calm, expanded, broad with the haughty breadth of the universe,
Old age, flowing free with the delicious near-by freedom of death.

Allons! to that which is endless as it was beginningless,
To undergo much, tramps of days, rests of nights,
To merge all in the travel they tend to, and the days and nights they tend to,
Again to merge them in the start of superior journeys,

To see nothing anywhere but what you may reach it and pass it,
To conceive no time, however distant, but what you may reach it and pass it,
To look up or down the road but it stretches and waits for you, however long but it stretches and waits for you,
To see no being, not God's or any, but you also go thither,
To see no possession but may possess it, enjoying all without labour or purchase, abstracting the feast yet not abstracting one particle of it,
To take the best of the farmer's farm and the rich man's elegant villa, and the chaste blessings of the well-married couple, and the fruits of orchards and flowers of gardens,
To take to your use out of the compact cities as you pass through,
To carry buildings and streets with you afterward where-ever you go,
To gather the minds of men out of their brains as you encounter them, to gather the love out of their hearts.
To take your lovers on the road with you, for all that you leave them behind you,
To know the universe itself as a road, as many roads, as roads for travelling souls.

All parts away for the progress of souls,
All religion, all solid things, arts, governments—all that was or is apparent upon this globe or any globe, falls into niches and corners before the procession of souls along the grand roads of the universe.

Of the progress of the souls of men and women along the grand roads of the universe, all other progress is the needed emblem and sustenance.

Forever alive, forever forward,
Stately, solemn, sad, withdrawn, baffled, mad, turbulent, feeble, dissatisfied,
Desperate, proud, fond, sick, accepted by men, rejected by men,
They go! they go! I know that they go, but I know not where they go,
But I know that they go toward the best—toward something great.

Whoever you are, come forth! or man or woman come forth!
You must not stay sleeping and dallying there in the house, though you built it, or though it has been built for you.

Out of the dark confinement! out from behind the screen!
It is useless to protest, I know all and expose it.

Behold through you as bad as the rest,
Through the laughter, dancing, dining, supping of people,
Inside of dresses and ornaments, inside of those wash'd and trimm'd faces,
Behold a secret silent loathing and despair.

No husband, no wife, no friend, trusted to hear the confession,
Another self, a duplicate of every one, skulking and hiding it goes,
Formless and wordless through the streets of the cities, polite and bland in the parlours,
In the cars of railroads, in steamboats, in the public assembly,
Home to the houses of men and women, at the table, in the bed-room, everywhere,
Smartly attired, countenance smiling, form upright, death under the breast-bones, hell under the skull-bones,
Under the broadcloth and gloves, under the ribbons and artificial flowers,
Keeping fair with the customs, speaking not a syllable of itself.
Speaking of anything else, but never of itself.

Allons! through struggles and wars!
The goal that was named cannot be countermanded.

Have the past struggles succeeded?
What has succeeded? yourself? your nation? Nature?
Now understand me well—it is provided in the essence of things that from any fruition of success, no matter what, shall come forth something to make a greater struggle necessary.

My call is the call of the battle, I nourish active rebellion,
He going with me must go well arm'd,
He going with me goes often with spare diet, poverty, angry enemies, desertions.

Allons! the road is before us!
It is safe—I have tried it—my own feet have tried it well—be not detain'd!

Let the paper remain on the desk unwritten, and the book on the shelf unopen'd!
Let the tools remain in the workshop! let the money remain unearn'd!
Let the school stand! mind not the cry of the teacher!
Let the preacher preach in his pulpit! let the lawyer plead in the court, and the judge expound the law.

Camerado, I will give you my hand!
I give you my love more precious than money,
I give you myself before preaching or law;
Will you give me yourself? will you come travel with me?
Shall we stick by each other as long as we live?

Walt Whitman.

Walking Tours

It must not be imagined that a walking tour, as some would have us fancy, is merely a better or worse way of seeing the country. There are many ways of seeing landscape quite as good; and none more vivid, in spite of canting dilettantes, than from a railway train. But landscape on a walking tour is quite accessory. He who is indeed of the brotherhood does not voyage in quest of the picturesque, but of certain jolly humours—of the hope and spirit with which the march begins at morning, and the peace and spiritual repletion of the evening's rest. He cannot tell whether he puts his knapsack on, or takes it off, with more delight. The excitement of the departure puts him in key for that of the arrival. Whatever he does is not only a reward in itself, but will be further rewarded in the sequel; and so pleasure leads on to pleasure in an endless chain. It is this that so few can understand; they will either be always lounging or always at five miles an hour; they do not play off the one against the other, prepare all day for the evening, and all evening for the next day. And, above all, it is here that your overwalker fails of comprehension. His heart rises against those who drink their curaçoa in liqueur glasses, when he himself can swill it in a brown john. He will not believe that the flavour is more delicate in the smaller dose. He will not believe that to walk this unconscionable distance is merely to stupefy and brutalise himself, and come to his inn, at night, with a sort of frost on his five wits, and a starless night of darkness in his spirit. Not for him the mild luminous evening of the temperate walker! He has nothing left of man but a physical need for bedtime and a double nightcap; and even his pipe, if he be a smoker, will be savourless and disenchanted. It is the fate of such an one to take twice as much trouble as is needed to obtain happiness, and miss the happiness in the end; he is the man of the proverb, in short, who goes further and fares worse.

Now, to be properly enjoyed, a walking tour should be gone upon alone. If you go in a company, or even in pairs, it is no longer a walking tour in anything but name; it is something else and more in the nature of a picnic. A walking tour should be gone upon alone, because freedom is of the essence; because you should be able to stop and go on, and follow this way or that, as the freak takes you; and because you must have your own pace, and neither trot alongside a champion walker, nor mince in time with a girl. And then you must be open to all impressions and let your thoughts take colour from what you see. You should be as a pipe for any wind to play upon. "I cannot see the wit," says Hazlitt, "of walking and talking at the same time. When I am in the country, I wish to vegetate like the country," which is the gist of all that can be said upon the matter. There should be no cackle of voices at your elbow, to jar on the meditative silence of the morning. And so long as a man is reasoning he cannot surrender himself to that fine intoxication that comes of much motion in the open air, that begins in a sort of dazzle and sluggishness of the brain, and ends in a peace that passes comprehension.

During the first day or so of any tour there are moments of bitterness, when the traveller feels more than coldly towards his knapsack, when he is half in a mind to throw it bodily over the hedge and, like Christian on a similar occasion, "give three leaps and go on singing." And yet it soon acquires a property of easiness. It becomes magnetic; the spirit of the journey enters into it. And no sooner have you passed the straps over your shoulder than the lees of sleep are cleared from you, you pull yourself together with a shake, and fall at once into your stride. And surely, of all possible moods, this, in which a man takes the road, is the best. Of course, if he *will* keep thinking of his anxieties, if he *will* open the merchant Abudah's chest and walk arm in arm with the hag—why, wherever he is, and whether he walk fast or slow, the chances are that he will not be happy. And so much the more shame to himself! There are perhaps thirty men setting forth at that same hour, and I would lay a large wager there is not another dull face among the thirty. It would be a fine thing to follow, in a coat of darkness, one after another of these wayfarers, some summer morning, for the first few miles upon the road. This one, who walks fast, with a keen look in his eyes, is all concentrated in his own mind; he is up at his loom, weaving and weaving, to set the landscape to words. This one peers about, as he goes, among the grasses; he waits by the canal to watch the dragon-flies; he leans on the gate of the pasture, and cannot look enough upon the complacent kine. And here comes another talking, laughing, and gesticulating to himself. His face changes from time to time, as indignation flashes from his eyes or anger clouds his forehead. He is composing articles, delivering orations, and conducting the most impassioned interviews, by the way. A little farther on, and it is as like as not he will begin to sing. And well for him, supposing him to be no great master in that art, if he stumble across no stolid peasant at a corner; for on such an occasion, I scarcely know which is the more troubled, or whether it is worse to suffer the confusion of your troubadour or the unfeigned alarm of your clown. A sedentary population, accustomed, besides, to the strange mechanical bearing of the common tramp, can in no wise explain to itself the gaiety of these passers-by. I knew one man who was arrested as a runaway lunatic, because, although a full-grown person with a red beard, he skipped as he went like a child. And you would be astonished if I were to tell you all the grave and learned heads who have confessed to me that, when on walking tours, they sang—and sang very ill—and had a pair of red ears when, as described above, the inauspicious peasant plumped into their arms from round a corner. And here, lest you think I am exaggerating, is Hazlitt's own confession, from his essay "On going a Journey," which is so good that there should be a tax levied on all who have not read it:—

"Give me the clear blue sky over my head," says he, "and the green turf beneath my feet, a winding road before me, and a three hours' march to dinner—and then to thinking! It is hard if I cannot start some game on these lone heaths. I laugh, I run, I leap, I sing for joy."

Bravo! After that adventure of my friend with the policeman, you would not have cared, would you, to publish that in the first person? But we have no bravery nowadays, and, even in books, must all pretend to be as dull and foolish as our neighbours. It was not so with Hazlitt. And notice how learned he is (as, indeed, throughout the essay) in the theory of walking tours. He is none of your athletic men in purple stockings, who walk their fifty miles a day: three hours' march is his ideal. And then he must have a winding road, the epicure!

Yet there is one thing I object to in these words of his, one thing in the great master's practice that seems to me not wholly wise. I do not approve of that leaping and running. Both of these hurry the respiration; they both shake up the brain out of its glorious open-air confusion; and they both break the pace. Uneven walking is not so agreeable to the body, and it distracts and irritates the mind. Whereas, when once you have fallen into an equable stride, it requires no conscious thought from you to keep it up, and yet it prevents you from thinking earnestly of anything else. Like knitting, like the work of a copying clerk, it gradually neutralises and sets to sleep the serious activity of the mind. We can think of this or that, lightly and laughingly, as a child thinks, or as we think in a morning doze; we can make puns or puzzle out acrostics, and trifle in a thousand ways with words or rhymes; but when it comes to honest work, when we come to gather ourselves together for an effort, we may sound the trumpet as loud and long as we please; the great barons of the mind will not rally to the standard, but sit, each one, at home, warming his hands over his own fire and brooding on his own private thought!

In the course of a day's walk, you see, there is much variance in the mood. From the exhilaration of the start, to the happy phlegm of the arrival, the change is certainly great. As the day goes on, the traveller moves from the one extreme towards the other. He becomes more and more incorporated with the material landscape, and the open-air drunkenness grows upon him with great strides, until he posts along the road, and sees everything about him, as in a cheerful dream. The first is certainly brighter, but the second stage is the more peaceful. A man does not make so many articles towards the end, nor does he laugh aloud; but the purely animal pleasures, the sense of physical well-being, the delight of every inhalation, of every time the muscles tighten down the thigh, console him for the absence of the others, and bring him to his destination still content.

Nor must I forget to say a word on bivouacs. You come to a milestone on a hill, or some place where deep ways meet under trees; and off goes the knapsack, and down you sit to smoke a pipe in the shade. You sink into yourself, and the birds come round and look at you, and your smoke dissipates upon the afternoon under the blue dome of heaven; and the sun lies warm upon your feet, and the cool air visits your neck and turns aside your open shirt. If you are not happy, you must have an evil conscience. You may dally as long as you like by the roadside. It is almost as if the millennium were arrived, when we shall throw our clocks and watches over the housetop, and remember time and seasons no more. Not to keep hours for a lifetime is, I was going to say, to live for ever. You have no idea, unless you have tried it, how endlessly long is a summer's day, that you measure out only by hunger, and bring to an end only when you are drowsy. I know a village where there are hardly any clocks, where no one knows more of the days of the week than by a sort of instinct for the *fête* on Sundays, and where only one person can tell you the day of the month, and she is generally wrong; and if people were aware how slow Time journeyed in that village, and what armfuls of spare hours he gives, over and above the bargain, to its wise inhabitants, I believe there would be a stampede out of London, Liverpool, Paris, and a variety of large towns, where the clocks lose their heads, and shake the hours out each one faster than the other, as though they were all in a wager. And all these foolish pilgrims would each bring his own misery along with him, in a watch-pocket! It is to be noticed, there were no clocks and watches in the much-vaunted days before the flood. It follows, of course, there were no appointments, and punctuality was not yet thought upon. "Though ye take from a covetous man all his treasure," says Milton, "he has yet one jewel left; ye cannot deprive him of his covetousness." And so I would say of a modern man of business, you may do what you will for him, put him in Eden, give him the elixir of life—he has still a flaw at heart, he still has his business habits. Now, there is no time when business habits are more mitigated than on a walking tour. And so during these halts, as I say, you will feel almost free.

But it is at night, and after dinner, that the best hour comes. There are no such pipes to be smoked as those that follow a good day's march; the flavour of the tobacco is a thing to be remembered, it is so dry and aromatic, so full and so fine. If you wind up the evening with grog, you will own there was never such grog; at every sip a jocund tranquillity spreads about your limbs, and sits easily in your heart. If you read a book—and you will never do so save by fits and starts—you find the language strangely racy and harmonious; words take a new meaning; single sentences possess the ear for half an hour together; and the writer endears himself to you, at every page, by the nicest coincidence of sentiment. It seems as if it were a book you had written yourself in a dream. To all we have read on such occasions we look back with special favour. "It was on the 10th of April 1798," says Hazlitt, with amorous precision, "that I sat down to a volume of the new *Heloïse*, at the Inn at Llangollen, over a bottle of sherry and a cold chicken." I should wish to quote more, for though we are mighty fine fellows nowadays, we cannot write like Hazlitt. And, talking of that, a volume of Hazlitt's essays would be a capital pocket-book on such a journey; so would a volume of Heine's songs; and for *Tristram Shandy* I can pledge a fair experience.

If the evening be fine and warm, there is nothing better in life than to lounge before the inn door in the sunset, or lean over the parapet of the bridge, to watch the weeds and the quick fishes. It is then, if ever, that you taste joviality to the full significance of that audacious word. Your muscles are so agreeably slack, you feel so clean and so strong and so idle, that whether you move or sit still, whatever you do is done with pride and a kingly sort of pleasure. You fall in talk with any one, wise or foolish, drunk or sober. And it seems as if a hot walk purged you, more than of anything else, of all narrowness and pride, and left curiosity to play its part freely, as in a child or a man of science. You lay aside all your own hobbies, to watch provincial humours develop themselves before you, now as a laughable farce, and now grave and beautiful like an old tale.

Or perhaps you are left to your own company for the night, and surly weather imprisons you by the fire. You may remember how Burns, numbering past pleasures, dwells upon the hours when he has been "happy thinking." It is a phrase that may well perplex a poor modern girt about on every side by clocks and chimes, and haunted, even at night, by flaming dial-plates. For we are all so busy, and have so many far-off projects to realise, and castles in the fire to turn into solid, habitable mansions on a gravel soil, that we can find no time for pleasure trips into the Land of Thought and among the Hills of Vanity. Changed times, indeed, when we must sit all night, beside the fire, with folded hands; and a changed world for most of us, when we find we can pass the hours without discontent, and be happy thinking. We are in such haste to be doing, to be writing, to be gathering gear, to make our voice audible a moment in the derisive silence of eternity, that we forget that one thing, of which these are but the parts—namely, to live. We fall in love, we drink hard, we run to and fro upon the earth like frightened sheep. And now you are to ask yourself if, when all is done, you would not have been better to sit by the fire at home, and be happy thinking. To sit still and contemplate,—to remember the faces of women without desire, to be pleased by the great deeds of men without envy, to be everything and everywhere in sympathy, and yet content to remain where and what you are—is not this to know both wisdom and virtue, and to dwell with happiness? After all, it is not they who carry flags, but they who look upon it from a private chamber, who have the fun of the procession. And once you are at that, you are in the very humour of all social heresy. It is no time for shuffling, or for big empty words. If you ask yourself what you mean by fame, riches, or learning, the answer is far to seek; and you go back into that kingdom of light imaginations, which seem so vain in the eyes of Philistines perspiring after wealth, and so momentous to those who are stricken with the disproportions of the world, and, in the face of the gigantic stars, cannot stop to split differences between two degrees of the infinitesimally small, such as a tobacco pipe or the Roman Empire, a million of money or a fiddlestick's end.

You lean from the window, your last pipe reeking whitely into the darkness, your body full of delicious pains, your mind enthroned in the seventh circle of content; when suddenly the mood changes, the weathercock goes about, and you ask yourself one question more: whether, for the interval, you have been the wisest philosopher or the most egregious of donkeys? Human experience is not yet able to reply; but at least you have had a fine moment, and looked down upon all the kingdoms of the earth. And whether it was wise or foolish, to-morrow's travel will carry you, body and mind, into some different parish of the infinite.

Robert Louis Stevenson.

Sylvanus Urban discovers a Good Brew

It must be nearly thirty years ago, long before the days of bicycles and motors, since Sylvanus Urban, then but a boy, passed over it. He had started from Chepstow on a solitary walking tour, and was soon caught in a rattling thunderstorm on the Wyndcliff. Tintern Abbey and Raglan Castle are fresh in his memory to-day. A mile or two out of Monmouth he came upon some excellent nutty-hearted ale, that George Borrow would have immortalised. As he pursued his way to Raglan Castle he pondered on the ale—"this way and that dividing the swift mind"—until at length, in despair of meeting an equal brew, he turned back again and had another tankard. Heavens, what days were those! In his pack he carried the *Essays of Elia* and read them in an old inn at Llandovery, where the gracious hostess lighted in his honour tall wax candles fit to stand before an altar. After leaving Llandovery, he lost his way among the Caermarthenshire hills, and was in very poor plight with hunger and fatigue when he reached the white-washed walls of Tregaron. At Harlech he rested for a couple of days, and then covered the way to Beddgelert—twenty miles, if he remembers rightly—at a spanking pace; proceeding in the late afternoon to climb Snowdon, and arriving at Llanberis an hour or so before midnight. Back to London, every inch of the way, walked the young Sylvanus. He indulges the hope that he may yet shoulder his pack again.

Gentleman's Magazine.

Minchmoor

Now that everybody is out of town, and every place in the guidebooks is as well known as Princes Street or Pall-Mall, it is something to discover a hill everybody has not been to the top of, and which is not in *Black*. Such a hill is *Minchmoor*, nearly three times as high as Arthur's Seat, and lying between Tweed and Yarrow.

The best way to ascend it is from Traquair. You go up the wild old Selkirk road, which passes almost right over the summit, and by which Montrose and his cavaliers fled from Philiphaugh, where Sir Walter's mother remembered crossing, when a girl, in a coach-and-six, on her way to a ball at Peebles, several footmen marching on either side of the carriage to prop it up or drag it out of the moss *haggs*; and where, to our amazement, we learned that the Duchess of Buccleuch had lately driven her ponies. Before this we had passed the grey, old-world entrance to Traquair House, and looked down its grassy and untrod avenue to the pallid, forlorn mansion, stricken all o'er with eld, and noticed the wrought-iron gate embedded in a foot deep and more of soil, never having opened since the '45. There are the huge Bradwardine bears on each side—most grotesque supporters—with a superfluity of ferocity and canine teeth. The whole place, like the family whose it has been, seems dying out—everything subdued to settled desolation. The old race, the old religion, the gaunt old house, with its small, deep, comfortless windows, the decaying trees, the stillness about the doors, the grass overrunning everything, nature reinstating herself in her quiet way—all this makes the place look as strange and pitiful among its fellows in the vale as would the Earl who built it three hundred years ago if we met him tottering along our way in the faded dress of his youth; but it looks the Earl's house still, and has a dignity of its own.

We soon found the Minchmoor road, and took at once to the hill, the ascent being, as often is with other ascents in this world, steepest at first. Nothing could be more beautiful than the view as we ascended, and got a look of the "eye-sweet" Tweed hills, and their "silver stream." It was one of the five or six good days of this summer—in early morning, "soft" and doubtful; but the mists drawing up, and now the noble, tawny hills were dappled with gleams and shadows—

"Sunbeams upon distant hills gliding apace"—

the best sort of day for mountain scenery—that ripple of light and shadow brings out the forms and the depths of the hills far better than a cloudless sky; and the horizon is generally wider.

Before us and far away was the round flat head of Minchmoor, with a dark, rich bloom on it from the thick, short heather—the hills around being green. Near the top, on the Tweed side, its waters trotting away cheerily to the glen at Bold, is the famous *Cheese Well*—always full, never overflowing. Here every traveler—Duchess, shepherd, or houseless *mugger*—stops, rests, and is thankful; doubtless so did Montrose, poor fellow, and his young nobles and their jaded steeds, on their scurry from Lesly and his Dragoons. It is called the Cheese Well from those who rest there dropping in bits of their provisions, as votive offerings to the fairies whose especial haunt this mountain was. After our rest and drink, we left the road and made for the top. When there we were well rewarded. The great round-backed, kindly, solemn hills of Tweed, Yarrow, and Ettrick lay all about like sleeping mastiffs—too plain to be grand, too ample and beautiful to be commonplace.

There, to the north-east, is the place—*Williamhope* ridge—where Sir Walter Scott bade farewell to his heroic friend Mungo Park. They had come up from *Ashestiel*, where Scott then lived, and where *Marmion* was written and its delightful epistles inspired— where he passed the happiest part of his life—leaving it, as Hogg said, "for gude an' a'"; for his fatal "dreams about his cottage" were now begun. He was to have "a hundred acres, two spare bed-rooms, with dressing rooms, each of which will on a pinch have a couch-bed." We all know what the dream, and the cottage, and the hundred acres came to—the ugly Abbotsford; the over-burdened, shattered brain driven wild, and the end, death, and madness. Well, it was on the ridge that the two friends—each romantic, but in such different ways—parted never to meet again. There is the ditch Park's horse stumbled over and all but fell. "I am afraid, Mungo, that's a bad omen," said the Sheriff; to which he answered, with a bright smile on his handsome, fearless face—"*Freits* (omens) follow those who look to them." With this expression, he struck the spurs into his horse, and Scott never saw him again. He had not long been married to a lovely and much-loved woman, and had been speaking to Scott about his new African scheme, and how he meant to tell his family he had some business in Edinburgh—send them his blessing, and be off—alas! never to return! Scott used to say, when speaking of this parting, "I stood and looked back, but he did not." A more memorable place for two such men to part in would not easily be found.

Where we are standing is the spot Scott speaks of when writing to Joanna Baillie about her new tragedies—"Were it possible for me to hasten the treat I expect in such a composition with you, I would promise to read the volume *at the silence of noonday upon the top of Minchmoor*. The hour is allowed, by those skilful in demonology, *to be as full of witching* as midnight itself; and I assure you I have felt really oppressed with a sort of fearful loneliness when looking around the naked towering ridges of desolate barrenness, which is all the eye takes in from the top of such a mountain, the patches of cultivation being hidden in the little glens, or only appearing to make one feel how feeble and ineffectual man has been to contend with the genius of the soil. It is in such a scene that the unknown and gifted author of *Albania* places the superstition which consists in hearing the noise of a chase, the baying of the hounds, the throttling sobs of the deer, the wild hollos of the huntsmen, and the 'hoof thick beating on the hollow hill.' I have often repeated his verses with some sensations of awe, in this place." The lines—and they are noble, and must have sounded wonderful with his voice and look—are as follows. Can no one tell us anything more of their author?—

> "There oft is heard, at midnight, or at noon,
> Beginning faint, but rising still more loud,
> And nearer, voice of hunters, and of hounds;
> And horns, hoarse-winded, blowing far and keen!
> Forthwith the hubbub multiplies; the gale
> Labours with wilder shrieks, and rifer din
> Of hot pursuit; the broken cry of deer
> Mangled by throttling dogs; the shouts of men,
> And hoofs thick beating on the hollow hill.
> Sudden the grazing heifer in the vale
> Starts at the noise, and both the herdman's ears
> Tingle with inward dread—aghast he eyes
> The mountain's height, and all the ridges round,
> Yet not one trace of living wight discerns,
> Nor knows, o'erawed and trembling as he stands,
> To what or whom he owes his idle fear—
> To ghost, to witch, to fairy, or to fiend;
> But wonders, and no end of wondering finds."

We listened for the hunt, but could only hear the wind sobbing from the blind "*Hopes*."[3]

The view from the top reaches from the huge *Harestane Broadlaw*—nearly as high as Ben Lomond—whose top is as flat as a table, and would make a race-course of two miles, and where the clouds are still brooding, to the *Cheviot*; and from the *Maiden Paps* in Liddesdale, and that wild huddle of hills at *Moss Paul*, to *Dunse Law*, and the weird *Lammermoors*. There is *Ruberslaw*, always surly and dark. The *Dunion*, beyond which lies Jedburgh. There are the *Eildons*, with their triple heights; and you can get a glimpse of the upper woods of Abbotsford, and the top of the hill above Cauldshiels Loch, that very spot where the "wondrous potentate,"—when suffering from languor and pain, and beginning to break down under his prodigious fertility,—composed those touching lines:—

"The sun upon the Weirdlaw Hill
In Ettrick's vale is sinking sweet;
The westland wind is hushed and still;
The lake lies sleeping at my feet.
Yet not the landscape to mine eye
Bears those bright hues that once it bore,
Though evening, with her richest dye,
Flames o'er the hills of Ettrick's shore.

With listless look along the plain
I see Tweed's silver current glide,
And coldly mark the holy fane
Of Melrose rise in ruined pride.
The quiet lake, and balmy air,
The hill, the stream, the tower, the tree,
Are they still such as once they were,
Or is the dreary change in me?

Alas! the warped and broken board,
How can it bear the painter's dye!
The harp of strained and tuneless chord,
How to the minstrel's skill reply!
To aching eyes each landscape lowers,
To feverish pulse each gale blows chill;

---

[3] The native word for hollows in the hills: thus, Dryhope, Gameshope, Chapelhope, &c.

> And Araby or Eden's bowers
> Were barren as this moorland hill."

There, too, is *Minto Hill*, as modest and shapely and smooth as Clytie's shoulders, and *Earlston Black Hill*, with Cowdenknowes at its foot; and there, standing stark and upright as a warder, is the stout old *Smailholme Tower*, seen and seeing all around. It is quite curious how unmistakable and important it looks at what must be twenty and more miles. It is now ninety years since that "lonely infant," who has sung its awful joys, was found in a thunderstorm, as we all know, lying on the soft grass at the foot of the grey old Strength, clapping his hands at each flash, and shouting, "Bonny! bonny!"

We now descended into Yarrow, and forgathered with a shepherd who was taking his lambs over to the great Melrose fair. He was a fine specimen of a border herd—young, tall, sagacious, self-contained, and free in speech and air. We got his heart by praising his dog *Jed*, a very fine collie, black and comely, gentle and keen—"Ay, she's a fell yin; she can do a' but speak." On asking him if the sheep dogs needed much teaching—"Whyles ay and whyles no; her kind (Jed's) needs nane. She sooks't in wi' her mither's milk." On asking him if the dogs were ever sold, he said—"Never, but at an orra time. Naebody wad sell a gude dowg, and naebody wad buy an ill ane." He told us with great feeling, of the death of one of his best dogs by poison. It was plainly still a grief to him. "What was he poisoned with?" "Strychnia," he said, as decidedly as might Dr Christison. "How do you know?" "I opened him, puir fallow, and got him analeezed!"

Now we are on Birkindale Brae, and are looking down on the same scene as did

> "James Boyd (the Earle of Arran, his brother was he),"

when he crossed Minchmoor on his way to deliver James the Fifth's message to

> "Yon outlaw Murray,
> Surely whaur bauldly bideth he."

> "Down Birkindale Brae when that he cam
> He saw the feir Foreste wi' his ee."

How James Boyd fared, and what the outlaw said, and what James and his nobles said and did, and how the outlaw at last made peace with his King, and rose up "Sheriffe of Ettricke Foreste," and how the bold ruffian boasted,

> "Fair Philiphaugh is mine by right,
> And Lewinshope still mine shall be;
> Newark, Foulshiels, and Tinnies baith
> My bow and arrow purchased me.
>
> And I have native steads to me
> The Newark Lee o' Hangingshaw.
> I have many steads in the Forest schaw,
> But them by name I dinna knaw."

And how King James snubbed

> "The kene Laird of Buckscleuth,
> A stalwart man and stern was he."

When the Laird hinted that,

> "For a king to gang an outlaw till
> Is beneath his state and dignitie.
> The man that wins yon forest intill
> He lives by reif and felony."
>
> "Then out and spak the nobil King,
> And round him cast a wilie ee.
>
> 'Now haud thy tongue, Sir Walter Scott,
> Nor speak o' reif or felonie—
> *For, had every honest man his awin kye,*
> *A richt puir clan thy name wud be!*'"

(by-the-bye, why did Professor Aytoun leave out this excellent hit in his edition?)—all this and much more may you see if you take up *The Border Minstrelsy*, and read "The Song of the Outlaw Murray," with the incomparable notes of Scott. But we are now well down the hill. There to the left, in the hollow, is *Permanscore*, where the King and the outlaw met:—

> "Bid him mete me at Permanscore,
> And bring four in his companie;
> Five Erles sall cum wi' mysel',
> Gude reason I sud honoured be."

And there goes our Shepherd with his long swinging stride. As different from his dark, wily companion, the Badenoch drover, as was Harry Wakefield from Robin Oig; or as the big, sunny Cheviot is from the lowering Ruberslaw; and there is *Jed* trotting meekly behind him—may she escape strychnia, and, dying at the fireside among the children, be laid like

> "Paddy Tims—whose soul at aise is—
> With the point of his nose
> And the tips of his toes
> Turn'd up to the roots of the daisies"—

unanaleezed, save by the slow cunning of the grave. And may her master get the top price for his lambs!

Do you see to the left that little plantation on the brow of Foulshiels Hill, with the sunlight lying on its upper corner? If you were there you might find among the brackens and foxglove a little headstone with "I. T." rudely carved on it. That is *Tibbie Tamson's grave*, known and feared all the country round.

This poor outcast was a Selkirk woman, who, under the stress of spiritual despair—that sense of perdition, which, as in Cowper's case, often haunts and overmasters the deepest and gentlest natures, making them think themselves

> "Damn'd below Judas, more abhorred than he was,"—

committed suicide; and being, with the gloomy, cruel superstition of the time, looked on by her neighbours as accursed of God, she was hurried into a rough white deal coffin, and carted out of the town, the people stoning it all the way till it crossed the Ettrick. Here, on this wild hillside, it found its rest, being buried where three lairds' lands meet. May we trust that the light of God's reconciled countenance has for all these long years been resting on that once forlorn soul, as His blessed sunshine now lies on her moorland grave! For "the mountains shall depart, and the hills be removed; but my kindness shall not depart from thee, neither shall the covenant of my peace be removed, saith the Lord that hath mercy on thee."

Now, we see down into the Yarrow—there is the famous stream twinkling in the sun. What stream and valley was ever so be-sung! You wonder at first why this has been, but the longer you look the less you wonder. There is a charm about it—it is not easy to say what. The huge sunny hills in which it is embosomed give it a look at once gentle and serious. They are great, and their gentleness makes them greater. Wordsworth has the right words, "pastoral melancholy"; and besides, the region is "not uninformed with phantasy and looks that threaten the profane"—the Flowers of Yarrow, the Douglas Tragedy, the Dowie Dens, Wordsworth's Yarrow Unvisited, Visited, and Re-Visited, and, above all, the glamour of Sir Walter, and Park's fatal and heroic story. Where can you find eight more exquisite lines anywhere than Logan's, which we all know by heart:—

> "His mother from the window looked,
> With all the longing of a mother;
> His little sister, weeping, walked
> The greenwood path to meet her brother.
> They sought him east, they sought him west,
> They sought him all the forest thorough—
> They only saw the cloud of night,
> They only heard the roar of Yarrow."

And there is *Newark Tower* among the rich woods; and *Harehead*, that cosiest, loveliest, and hospitablest of nests. Methinks I hear certain young voices among the hazels; out they come on the little haugh by the side of the deep, swirling stream, *fabulosus* as was ever Hydaspes. There they go "running races in their mirth," and is not that—*an me ludit amabilis insania?*—the voice of *ma pauvre petite*—*animosa infans*—the wilful, rich-eyed, delicious Eppie?

> "Oh blessed vision, happy child,
> Thou art so exquisitely wild!"

And there is *Black Andro and Glowr owr'em* and *Foulshiels*, where Park was born and bred; and there is the deep pool in the Yarrow where Scott found him plunging one stone after another into the water, and watching anxiously the bubbles as they rose to the surface. "This," said Scott to him, "appears but an idle amusement for one who has seen so much adventure." "Not so idle, perhaps, as you suppose," answered Mungo, "this was the way I used to ascertain the depth of a river in Africa." He was then meditating his second journey, but had said so to no one.

We go down by *Broadmeadows*, now held by that Yair "Hoppringle"—who so well governed Scinde—and into the grounds of Bowhill, and passing *Philiphaugh*, see where stout David Lesly crossed in the mist at daybreak with his heavy dragoons, many of them old soldiers of Gustavus, and routed the gallant Graeme; and there is *Slainmens Lee*, where the royalists lie; and there is *Carterhaugh*, the scene of the strange wild story of *Tamlane* and Lady Janet, when

> "She prinked hersell and prinned hersell
> By the ae light of the moon,
> And she's awa' to Carterhaugh
> To speak wi' young Tamlane."

Noel Paton might paint that night, when

> "'Twixt the hours of twelve and yin
> A north wind *tore the bent*";

when "fair Janet" in her green mantle

> "—— heard strange elritch sounds
> Upon the wind that went."

And straightway

> "About the dead hour o' the night
> She heard the bridles ring;
> Their oaten pipes blew wondrous shrill,
> The hemlock small blew clear;
> And louder notes from hemlock large
> And bog reed, struck the ear,"

and then the fairy cavalcade swept past, while Janet, filled with love and fear, looked out for the milk-white steed, and "gruppit it fast," and "pu'd the rider doon," the young Tamlane, whom, after dipping "in a stand of milk and then in a stand of water,"

> "She wrappit ticht in her green mantle,
> And sae her true love won!"

This ended our walk. We found the carriage at the Philiphaugh home-farm, and we drove home by *Yair* and *Fernilee*, *Ashestiel* and *Elibank*, and passed the bears as ferocious as ever, "the orange sky of evening" glowing through their wild tusks, the old house looking even older in the fading light. And is not this a walk worth making? One of our number had been at the Land's End and Johnnie Groat's, and now on Minchmoor; and we wondered how many other men had been at all the three, and how many had enjoyed Minchmoor more than he.

Dr John Brown.

In Praise of Walking

As a man grows old, he is told by some moralists that he may find consolation for increasing infirmities in looking back upon a well-spent life. No doubt such a retrospect must be very agreeable, but the question must occur to many of us whether our life offers the necessary materials for self-complacency. What part of it, if any, has been well spent? To that I find it convenient to reply, for my own purposes, any part in which I thoroughly enjoyed myself. If it be proposed to add "innocently," I will not quarrel with the amendment. Perhaps, indeed, I may have a momentary regret for some pleasures which do not quite deserve that epithet, but the pleasure of which I am about to speak is obtrusively and pre-eminently innocent. Walking is among recreations what ploughing and fishing are among industrial labours: it is primitive and simple; it brings us into contact with mother earth and unsophisticated nature; it requires no elaborate apparatus and no extraneous excitement. It is fit even for poets and philosophers, and he who can thoroughly enjoy it must have at least some capacity for worshipping the "cherub Contemplation." He must be able to enjoy his own society without the factitious stimulants of the more violent physical recreations. I have always been a humble admirer of athletic excellence. I retain, in spite of much head-shaking from wise educationalists, my early veneration for the heroes of the river and the cricket-field. To me they have still the halo which surrounded them in the days when "muscular Christianity" was first preached and the whole duty of man said to consist in fearing God and walking a thousand miles in a thousand hours. I rejoice unselfishly in these later days to see the stream of bicyclists restoring animation to deserted highroads or to watch even respected contemporaries renewing their youth in the absorbing delights of golf. While honouring all genuine delight in manly exercises, I regret only the occasional admixture of lower motives which may lead to its degeneration. Now it is one merit of walking that its real devotees are little exposed to such temptations. Of course there are such things as professional pedestrians making "records" and seeking the applause of the mob. When I read of the immortal Captain Barclay performing his marvellous feats, I admire respectfully, but I fear that his motives included a greater admixture of vanity than of the emotions congenial to the higher intellect. The true walker is one to whom the pursuit is in itself delightful; who is not indeed priggish enough to be above a certain complacency in the physical prowess required for his pursuit, but to whom the muscular effort of the legs is subsidiary to the "cerebration" stimulated by the effort; to the quiet musings and imaginings which arise most spontaneously as he walks, and generate the intellectual harmony which is the natural accompaniment to the monotonous tramp of his feet. The cyclist or the golf-player, I am told, can hold such intercourse with himself in the intervals of striking the ball or working his machine. But the true pedestrian loves walking because, so far from distracting his mind, it is favourable to the equable and abundant flow of tranquil and half-conscious meditation. Therefore I should be sorry if the pleasures of cycling or any other recreation tended to put out of fashion the habit of the good old walking tour.

For my part, when I try to summon up remembrance of "well-spent" moments, I find myself taking a kind of inverted view of the past; inverted, that is, so far as the accidental becomes the essential. If I turn over the intellectual album which memory is always compiling, I find that the most distinct pictures which it contains are those of old walks. Other memories of incomparably greater intrinsic value coalesce into wholes. They are more massive but less distinct. The memory of a friendship that has brightened one's whole life survives not as a series of incidents but as a general impression of the friend's characteristic qualities due to the superposition of innumerable forgotten pictures. I remember him, not the specific conversations by which he revealed himself. The memories of walks, on the other hand, are all localised and dated; they are hitched on to particular times and places; they spontaneously form a kind of calendar or connecting thread upon which other memories may be strung. As I look back, a long series of little vignettes presents itself, each representing a definite stage of my earthly pilgrimage summed up and embodied in a walk. Their background of scenery recalls places once familiar, and the thoughts associated with the places revive thoughts of the contemporary occupations. The labour of scribbling books happily leaves no distinct impression, and I would forget that it had ever been undergone; but the picture of some delightful ramble includes incidentally a reference to the nightmare of literary toil from which it relieved me. The author is but the accidental appendage of the tramp. My days are bound each to each not by "natural piety" (or not, let me say, by natural piety alone) but by pedestrian enthusiasm. The memory of school days, if one may trust to the usual reminiscences, generally clusters round a flogging, or some solemn words from the spiritual teacher instilling the seed of a guiding principle of life. I remember a sermon or two rather ruefully; and I confess to memories of a flogging so unjust that I am even now stung by the thought of it. But what comes most spontaneously to my mind is the memory of certain strolls, "out of bounds," when I could forget the Latin grammar, and enjoy such a sense of the beauties of nature as is embodied for a child in a pond haunted by water-rats, or a field made romantic by threats of "mantraps and spring-guns." Then, after a crude fashion, one was becoming more or less of a reflecting and individual being, not a mere automaton set in movement by pedagogic machinery.

The day on which I was fully initiated into the mysteries is marked by a white stone. It was when I put on a knapsack and started from Heidelberg for a march through the Odenwald. Then I first knew the delightful sensation of independence and detachment enjoyed during a walking tour. Free from all bothers of railway time-tables and extraneous machinery, you trust to your own legs, stop when you please, diverge into any track that takes your fancy, and drop in upon some quaint variety of human life at every inn where you put up for the night. You share for the time the mood in which Borrow settled down in the dingle after escaping from his bondage in the publishers' London slums. You have no dignity to support, and the dress-coat of conventional life has dropped into oblivion, like the bundle from Christian's shoulders. You are in the world of Lavengro, and would be prepared to take tea with Miss Isopel Berners or with the Welsh preacher who thought that he had committed the unpardonable sin. Borrow, of course, took the life more seriously than the literary gentleman who is only escaping on ticket-of-leave from the prison-house of respectability, and is quite unequal to a personal conflict with "blazing Bosville"—the flaming tinman. He is only dipping in the element where his model was thoroughly at home. I remember, indeed, one figure in that first walk which I associate with Benedict Moll, the strange treasure-seeker whom Borrow encountered in his Spanish rambles. My acquaintance was a mild German innkeeper, who sat beside me on a bench while I was trying to assimilate certain pancakes, the only dinner he could provide, still fearful in memory, but just attackable after a thirty-miles' tramp. He confided to me that, poor as he was, he had discovered the secret of perpetual motion. He kept his machine upstairs, where it discharged the humble duty of supplying the place of a shoe-black; but he was about to go to London to offer it to a British capitalist. He looked wistfully at me as possibly a capitalist in (very deep) disguise, and I thought it wise to evade a full explanation. I have not been worthy to encounter many of such quaint incidents and characters as seem to have been normal in Borrow's experience; but the first walk, commonplace enough, remains distinct in my memory. I kept no journal, but I could still give the narrative day by day—the sights which I dutifully admired and the very state of my bootlaces. Walking tours thus rescue a bit of one's life from oblivion. They play in one's personal recollections the part of those historical passages in which Carlyle is an unequalled master; the little islands of light in the midst of the darkening gloom of the past, on which you distinguish the actors in some old drama actually alive and moving. The devotee of other athletic sports remembers special incidents: the occasion on which he hit a cricket-ball over the pavilion at Lord's, or the crab which he caught as his boat was shooting Barnes Bridge. But those are memories of exceptional moments of glory or the reverse, and apt to be tainted by vanity or the spirit of competition. The walks are the unobtrusive connecting thread of other memories, and yet each walk is a little drama in itself, with a definite plot with episodes and catastrophes, according to the requirements of Aristotle; and it is naturally interwoven with all the thoughts, the friendships, and the interests that form the staple of ordinary life.

Walking is the natural recreation for a man who desires not absolutely to suppress his intellect but to turn it out to play for a season. All great men of letters have, therefore, been enthusiastic walkers (exceptions, of course, excepted). Shakespeare, besides being a sportsman, a lawyer, a divine, and so forth, conscientiously observed his own maxim, "Jog on, jog on, the footpath way"; though a full proof of this could only be given in an octavo volume. Anyhow, he divined the connection between walking and a "merry heart"; that is, of course, a cheerful acceptance of our position in the universe founded upon the deepest moral and philosophical principles. His friend, Ben Jonson, walked from London to Scotland. Another gentleman of the period (I forget his name) danced from London to Norwich. Tom Coryate hung up in his parish church the shoes in which he walked from Venice and then started to walk (with occasional lifts) to India. Contemporary walkers of more serious character might be quoted, such as the admirable Barclay, the famous Quaker apologist, from whom the great Captain Barclay inherited his prowess. Every one, too, must remember the incident in Walton's *Life of Hooker*. Walking from Oxford to Exeter, Hooker went to see his godfather, Bishop Jewel, at

Salisbury. The Bishop said that he would lend him "a horse which hath carried me many a mile, and, I thank God, with much ease," and "presently delivered into his hands a walking staff with which he professed he had travelled through many parts of Germany." He added ten groats and munificently promised ten groats more when Hooker should restore the "horse." When, in later days, Hooker once rode to London, he expressed more passion than that mild divine was ever known to show upon any other occasion against a friend who had dissuaded him from "footing it." The hack, it seems, "trotted when he did not," and discomposed the thoughts which had been soothed by the walking staff. His biographer must be counted, I fear, among those who do not enjoy walking without the incidental stimulus of sport. Yet the *Compleat Angler* and his friends start by a walk of twenty good miles before they take their "morning draught." Swift, perhaps, was the first person to show a full appreciation of the moral and physical advantages of walking. He preached constantly upon this text to Stella, and practised his own advice. It is true that his notions of a journey were somewhat limited. Ten miles a day was his regular allowance when he went from London to Holyhead, but then he spent time in lounging at wayside inns to enjoy the talk of the tramps and ostlers. The fact, though his biographers are rather scandalised, shows that he really appreciated one of the true charms of pedestrian expeditions. Wesley is generally credited with certain moral reforms, but one secret of his power is not always noticed. In his early expeditions he went on foot to save horse hire, and made the great discovery that twenty or thirty miles a day was a wholesome allowance for a healthy man. The fresh air and exercise put "spirit into his sermons," which could not be rivalled by the ordinary parson of the period, who too often passed his leisure lounging by his fireside. Fielding points the contrast. Trulliber, embodying the clerical somnolence of the day, never gets beyond his pig-sties, but the model Parson Adams steps out so vigorously that he distances the stagecoach, and disappears in the distance rapt in the congenial pleasures of walking and composing a sermon. Fielding, no doubt, shared his hero's taste, and that explains the contrast between his vigorous naturalism and the sentimentalism of Richardson, who was to be seen, as he tells us, "stealing along from Hammersmith to Kensington with his eyes on the ground, propping his unsteady limbs with a stick." Even the ponderous Johnson used to dissipate his early hypochondria by walking from Lichfield to Birmingham and back (thirty-two miles), and his later melancholy would have changed to a more cheerful view of life could he have kept up the practice in his beloved London streets. The literary movement at the end of the eighteenth century was obviously due in great part, if not mainly, to the renewed practice of walking. Wordsworth's poetical autobiography shows how every stage in his early mental development was connected with some walk in the Lakes. The sunrise which startled him on a walk after a night spent in dancing first set him apart as a "dedicated spirit." His walking tour in the Alps—then a novel performance—roused him to his first considerable poem. His chief performance is the record of an excursion on foot. He kept up the practice, and De Quincey calculates somewhere what multiple of the earth's circumference he had measured on his legs, assuming, it appears, that he averaged ten miles a day. De Quincey himself, we are told, slight and fragile as he was, was a good walker, and would run up a hill "like a squirrel." Opium-eating is not congenial to walking, yet even Coleridge, after beginning the habit, speaks of walking forty miles a day in Scotland, and, as we all know, the great manifesto of the new school of poetry, the Lyrical Ballads, was suggested by the famous walk with Wordsworth, when the first stanzas of the *Ancient Mariner* were composed. A remarkable illustration of the wholesome influence might be given from the cases of Scott and Byron. Scott, in spite of his lameness, delighted in walks of twenty and thirty miles a day, and in climbing crags, trusting to the strength of his arms to remedy the stumblings of his foot. The early strolls enabled him to saturate his mind with local traditions, and the passion for walking under difficulties showed the manly nature which has endeared him to three generations. Byron's lameness was too severe to admit of walking, and therefore all the unwholesome humours which would have been walked off in a good cross-country march accumulated in his brain and caused the defects, the morbid affectation and perverse misanthropy, which half ruined the achievement of the most masculine intellect of his time.

It is needless to accumulate examples of a doctrine which will no doubt be accepted as soon as it is announced. Walking is the best of panaceas for the morbid tendencies of authors. It is, I need only observe, as good for reasoners as for poets. The name of "peripatetic" suggests the connection. Hobbes walked steadily up and down the hills in his patron's park when he was in his venerable old age. To the same practice may be justly ascribed the utilitarian philosophy. Old Jeremy Bentham kept himself up to his work for eighty years by his regular "post-jentacular circumgyrations." His chief disciple, James Mill, walked incessantly and preached as he walked. John Stuart Mill imbibed at once psychology, political economy, and a love of walks from his father. Walking was his one recreation; it saved him from becoming a mere smoke-dried pedant; and though he put forward the pretext of botanical researches, it helped him to perceive that man is something besides a mere logic machine. Mill's great rival as a spiritual guide, Carlyle, was a vigorous walker, and even in his latest years was a striking figure when performing his regular constitutionals in London. One of the vivid passages in the *Reminiscences* describes his walk with Irving from Glasgow to Drumclog. Here they sat on the "brow of a peat hag, while far, far away to the westward, over our brown horizon, towered up white and visible at the many miles of distance a high irregular pyramid. Ailsa Craig we at once guessed, and thought of the seas and oceans over yonder." The vision naturally led to a solemn conversation, which was an event in both lives. Neither Irving nor Carlyle himself feared any amount of walking in those days, it is added, and next day Carlyle took his longest walk, fifty-four miles. Carlyle is unsurpassable in his descriptions of scenery: from the pictures of mountains in *Sartor Resartus* to the battle-pieces in *Frederick*. Ruskin, himself a good walker, is more rhetorical but not so graphic; and it is self-evident that nothing educates an eye for the features of a landscape so well as the practice of measuring it by your own legs.

The great men, it is true, have not always acknowledged their debt to the genius, whoever he may be, who presides over pedestrian exercise. Indeed, they have inclined to ignore the true source of their impulse. Even when they speak of the beauties of nature, they would give us to understand that they might have been disembodied spirits, taking aerial flights among mountain solitudes, and independent of the physical machinery of legs and stomachs. When long ago the Alps cast their spell upon me, it was woven in a great degree by the eloquence of *Modern Painters*. I hoped to share Ruskin's ecstasies in a reverent worship of Mont Blanc and the Matterhorn. The influence of any cult, however, depends upon the character of the worshipper, and I fear that in this case the charm operated rather perversely. I stimulated a passion for climbing which absorbed my energies and distracted me from the prophet's loftier teaching. I might have followed him from the mountains to picture-galleries, and spent among the stones of Venice hours which I devoted to attacking hitherto unascended peaks and so losing my last chance of becoming an art critic. I became a fair judge of an Alpine guide, but I do not even know how to make a judicious allusion to Botticelli or Tintoretto. I can't say that I feel the smallest remorse. I had a good time, and at least escaped one temptation to talking nonsense. It follows, however, that my passion for the mountains had something earthly in its composition. It is associated with memories of eating and drinking. It meant delightful comradeship with some of the best of friends; but our end, I admit, was not always of the most exalted or æsthetic strain. A certain difficulty results. I feel an uncomfortable diffidence. I hold that Alpine walks are the poetry of the pursuit; I could try to justify the opinion by relating some of the emotions suggested by the great scenic effects: the sunrise on the snow fields; the storm-clouds gathering under the great peaks; the high pasturages knee-deep in flowers; the torrents plunging through the "cloven ravines," and so forth. But the thing has been done before, better than I could hope to do it; and when I look back at those old passages in *Modern Painters*, and think of the enthusiasm which prompted to exuberant sentences of three or four hundred words, I am not only abashed by the thought of their unapproachable eloquence, but feel as though they conveyed a tacit reproach. You, they seem to say, are, after all, a poor prosaic creature, affecting a love of sublime scenery as a cloak for more grovelling motives. I could protest against this judgment, but it is better at present to omit the topic, even though it would give the strongest groundwork for my argument.

Perhaps, therefore, it is better to trust the case for walking to where the external stimulus of splendours and sublimities is not so overpowering. A philosophic historian divides the world into the regions where man is stronger than nature and the regions where nature is stronger than man. The true charm of walking is most unequivocally shown when it is obviously dependent upon the walker himself. I became an enthusiast in the Alps, but I have found almost equal pleasure in walks such as one described by Cowper, where the view from a summit is bounded, not by Alps or Apennines, but by "a lofty quickset hedge." Walking gives a charm to the most commonplace British scenery. A love of walking not only makes any English county tolerable but seems to make the charm inexhaustible. I know only two or three districts minutely, but the more familiar I have become with any of them the more I have wished to return, to invent some new combination of old strolls or to inspect some hitherto unexplored nook. I love the English Lakes, and certainly not on account of associations. I cannot "associate." Much as I respect Wordsworth, I don't care to see the cottage in which he lived: it only suggests to me that anybody else might have lived there. There is an intrinsic charm about the Lake Country, and to me at least a music in the very names of Helvellyn and Skiddaw and Scawfell. But this may be due to the suggestion that it is a miniature of the Alps. I appeal, therefore, to the Fen Country, the country of which Alton Locke's farmer boasted that it had none of your "darned ups and downs" and "was as flat as his barn-door for forty miles on end." I used to climb the range of the Gogmagogs, to see the tower of Ely, some sixteen miles across the dead level, and I boasted that every term I devised a new route for walking to the cathedral from Cambridge. Many of these routes led by the little public-house called "Five Miles from Anywhere": which in my day was the Mecca to which a remarkable club, called—from the name of the village—the "Upware Republic," made periodic pilgrimages. What its members specifically did when they got there beyond consuming beer is unknown to me; but the charm was in the distance "from anywhere"—a sense of solitude under the great canopy of the heavens, where, like emblems of infinity,

"The trenched waters run from sky to sky."

I have always loved walks in the Fens. In a steady march along one of the great dykes by the monotonous canal with the exuberant vegetation dozing in its stagnant waters, we were imbibing the spirit of the scenery. Our talk might be of senior wranglers or the University crew, but we felt the curious charm of the great flats. The absence, perhaps, of definite barriers makes you realise that you are on the surface of a planet rolling through free and boundless space. One queer figure comes back to me—a kind of scholar-gipsy of the fens. Certain peculiarities made it undesirable to trust him with cash, and his family used to support him by periodically paying his score at riverside publics. They allowed him to print certain poems, moreover, which he would impart when one met him on the towpath. In my boyhood, I remember, I used to fancy that the most delightful of all lives must be that of a bargee—enjoying a perpetual picnic. This gentleman seemed to have carried out the idea; and in the intervals of lectures, I could fancy that he had chosen the better part. His poems, alas! have long vanished from my memory, and I therefore cannot quote what would doubtless have given the essence of the local sentiment and invested such names as Wicken Fen or Swaffham Lode with associations equal to those of Arnold's Hincksey ridge and Fyfield elm.

Another set of walks may, perhaps, appeal to more general sympathy. The voice of the sea, we know, is as powerful as the voice of the mountain; and, to my taste, it is difficult to say whether the Land's End is not in itself a more impressive station than the top of Mont Blanc. The solitude of the frozen peaks suggests tombstones and death. The sea is always alive and at work. The hovering gulls and plunging gannets and the rollicking porpoises are animating symbols of a gallant struggle with wind and wave. Even the unassociative mind has a vague sense of the Armada and Hakluyt's heroes in the background. America and Australia are just over the way. "Is not this a dull place?" asked some one of an old woman whose cottage was near to the Lizard lighthouse. "No," she replied, "it is so 'cosmopolitan.'" That was a simple-minded way of expressing the charm suggested in Milton's wonderful phrase:

"Where the great Vision of the guarded Mount
Looks towards Namancos and Bayona's hold."

She could mentally follow the great ships coming and going, and shake hands with people at the ends of the earth. The very sight of a fishing-boat, as painters seem to have found out, is a poem in itself. But is it not all written in *Westward Ho!* and in the *Prose Idylls*, in which Kingsley put his most genuine power? Of all walks that I have made, I can remember none more delightful than those round the south-western promontory. I have followed the coast at different times from the mouth of the Bristol Avon by the Land's End to the Isle of Wight, and I am only puzzled to decide which bay or cape is the most delightful. I only know that the most delightful was the more enjoyable when placed in its proper setting by a long walk. When you have made an early start, followed the coastguard track on the slopes above the cliffs, struggled through the gold and purple carpeting of gorse and heather on the moors, dipped down into quaint little coves with a primitive fishing village, followed the blinding whiteness of the sands round a lonely bay, and at last emerged upon a headland where you can settle into a nook of the rocks, look down upon the glorious blue of the Atlantic waves breaking into foam on the granite, and see the distant sea-levels glimmering away till they blend imperceptibly into cloudland; then you can consume your modest sandwiches, light your pipe, and feel more virtuous and thoroughly at peace with the universe than it is easy even to conceive yourself elsewhere. I have fancied myself on such occasions to be a felicitous blend of poet and saint—which is an agreeable sensation. What I wish to point out, however, is that the sensation is confined to the walker. I respect the cyclist, as I have said; but he is enslaved by his machine: he has to follow the highroad, and can only come upon what points of view open to the commonplace tourist. He can see nothing of the retired scenery which may be close to him, and cannot have his mind brought into due harmony by the solitude and by the long succession of lovely bits of scenery which stand so coyly aside from public notice.

The cockney cyclist who wisely seeks to escape at intervals from the region "where houses thick and sewers annoy the air," suffers the same disadvantages. To me, for many years, it was a necessity of life to interpolate gulps of fresh air between the periods of inhaling London fogs. When once beyond the "town" I looked out for notices that trespassers would be prosecuted. That gave a strong presumption that the trespass must have some attraction. The cyclist could only reflect that trespassing for him was not only forbidden but impossible. To me it was a reminder of the many delicious bits of walking which, even in the neighbourhood of London, await the man who has no superstitious reverence for legal rights. It is indeed surprising how many charming walks can be contrived by a judicious combination of a little trespassing with the rights of way happily preserved over so many commons and footpaths. London, it is true, goes on stretching its vast octopus arms farther into the country. Unlike the devouring dragon of Wantley, to whom "houses and churches" were like "geese and turkies," it spreads houses and churches over the fields of our childhood. And yet, between the great lines of railway there are still fields not yet desecrated by advertisements of liver pills. It is a fact that within twenty miles of London two travellers recently asked their way at a lonely farmhouse; and that the mistress of the house, seeing that they were far from an inn, not only gave them a seat and luncheon, but positively refused to accept payment. That suggested an idyllic state of society which, it is true, one must not count upon discovering. Yet hospitality, the virtue of primitive regions, has not quite vanished, it would appear, even from this over-civilised region. The travellers, perhaps, had something specially attractive in their manners. In that or some not distant ramble they made time run back for a couple of centuries. They visited the quiet grave where Penn lies under the shadow of the old Friends' meeting-house, and came to the cottage where the seat on which Milton talked to Ellwood about *Paradise Regained* seems to be still waiting for his return; and climbed the hill to the queer monument which records how Captain Cook demonstrated the goodness of Providence by disproving the existence of a continent in the South Sea—(the argument is too obvious to require exposition); and then gazed reverently upon the obelisk, not far off, which marks the point at which George III. concluded a famous stag hunt. A little valley in the quiet chalk country of Buckinghamshire leads past these and other memorials, and the lover of historical associations, with the help of Thorne's *Environs of London*, may add indefinitely to the list. I don't object to an association when it presents itself spontaneously and unobtrusively. It should not be the avowed goal but the accidental addition to the interest of a walk; and it is then pleasant to think of one's ancestors as sharers in the pleasures. The region enclosed within a radius of thirty miles from Charing Cross has charms enough even for the least historical of minds. You can't hold a fire in your hand, according to a high authority, by thinking on the frosty Caucasus; but I can comfort myself now and then, when the fellow-passengers who tread on my heels in London have put me out of temper, by thinking of Leith Hill. It only rises to the height of a thousand feet by help of the "Folly" on the top, but you can see, says my authority, twelve counties from the tower; and, if certain legendary ordnance surveyors spoke the truth, distinguish the English Channel to the south, and Dunstable Hill, far beyond London, to the north. The Crystal Palace, too, as we are assured, "sparkles like a diamond." That is gratifying; but to me the panorama suggests a whole network of paths, which have been the scene of personally conducted expeditions, in which I displayed the skill on which I most pride myself—skill, I mean, in devising judicious geographical combinations, and especially of contriving admirable short cuts. The persistence of some companions in asserting that my short cuts might be the longest way round shows that the best of men are not free from jealousy. Mine, at any rate, led me and my friends through pleasant places innumerable. My favourite passage in *Pilgrim's Progress*—an allegory which could have occurred, by the way, to no one who was not both a good man and a good walker—was always that in which Christian and Hopeful leave the highroad to cross a stile into "Bypath Meadow." I should certainly have approved the plan. The path led them, it is true, into the castle of Giant Despair; but the law of trespass has become milder; and the incident really added that spice of adventure which is delightful to the genuine pilgrim. We defied Giant Despair; and if our walks were not quite so edifying as those of Christian and his friends, they add a pleasant strand to the thread of memory which joins the past years. Conversation, we are often told, like letter-writing, is a lost art. We live too much in crowds. But if ever men can converse pleasantly, it is when they are invigorated by a good march: when the reserve is lowered by the long familiarity of a common pursuit, or when, if bored, you can quietly drop behind, or perhaps increase the pace sufficiently to check the breath of the persistent argufier.

Nowhere, at least, have I found talk flow so freely and pleasantly as in a march through pleasant country. And yet there is also a peculiar charm in the solitary expedition when your interlocutor must be yourself. That may be enjoyed, perhaps even best enjoyed, in London streets themselves. I have read somewhere of a distinguished person who composed his writings during such perambulations, and the statement was supposed to prove his remarkable power of intellectual concentration. My own experience would tend to diminish the wonder. I hopelessly envy men who can think consecutively under conditions distracting to others—in a crowded meeting or in the midst of their children—for I am as sensitive as most people to distraction; but if I can think at all, I am not sure that the roar of the Strand is not a more favourable environment than the quiet of my own study. The mind—one must only judge from one's own—seems to me to be a singularly ill-constructed apparatus. Thoughts are slippery things. It is terribly hard to keep them in the track presented by logic. They jostle each other, and suddenly skip aside to make room for irrelevant and accidental neighbours; till the stream of thought, of which people talk, resembles rather such a railway journey as one makes in dreams, where at every few yards you are shunted on to the wrong line. Now, though a London street is full of distractions, they become so multitudinous that they neutralise each other. The whirl of conflicting impulses becomes a continuous current because it is so chaotic and determines a mood of sentiment if not a particular vein of reflection. Wordsworth describes the influence upon himself in a curious passage of his *Prelude*. He wandered through London as a raw country lad, seeing all the sights from Bartholomew Fair to St Stephen's, and became a unit of the "monstrous ant-hill in a too busy world." Of course, according to his custom, he drew a moral, and a most excellent moral, from the bewildering complexity of his new surroundings. He learnt, it seems, to recognise the unity of man and to feel that the spirit of nature was upon him "in London's vast domain" as well as on the mountains. That comes of being a philosophical poet with a turn for optimism. I will not try to interpret or to comment, for I am afraid that I have not shared the emotions which he expresses. A cockney, born and bred, takes surroundings for granted. The hubbub has ceased to distract him; he is like the people who were said to become deaf because they always lived within the roar of a waterfall: he realises the common saying that the deepest solitude is solitude in a crowd; he derives a certain stimulus from a vague sympathy with the active life around him, but each particular stimulus remains, as the phrase goes, "below the threshold of consciousness." To some such effect, till psychologists will give me a better theory, I attribute the fact that what I please to call my "mind" seems to work more continuously and coherently in a street walk than elsewhere. This, indeed, may sound like a confession of cynicism. The man who should open his mind to the impressions naturally suggested by the "monstrous anthill" would be in danger of becoming a philanthropist or a pessimist, of being overpowered by thoughts of gigantic problems, or of the impotence of the individual to solve them. Carlyle, if I remember rightly, took Emerson round London in order to convince his optimistic friend that the devil was still in full activity. The gates of hell might be found in every street. I remember how, when coming home from a country walk on a sweltering summer night, and seeing the squalid population turning out for a gasp of air in their only playground, the vast labyrinth of hideous lanes, I seemed to be in Thomson's *City of Dreadful Night*. Even the vanishing of quaint old nooks is painful when one's attention is aroused. There is a certain churchyard wall, which I pass sometimes, with an inscription to commemorate the benefactor who erected it "to keep out the pigs." I regret the pigs and the village green which they presumably imply. The heart, it may be urged, must be hardened not to be moved by many such texts for melancholy reflection. I will not argue the point. None of us can be always thinking over the riddle of the universe, and I confess that my mind is generally employed on much humbler topics. I do not defend my insensibility nor argue that London walks are the best. I only maintain that even in London, walking has a peculiar fascination. The top of an omnibus is an excellent place for meditation; but it has not, for me at least, that peculiar hypnotic influence which seems to be favourable to thinking, and to pleasant daydreaming when locomotion is carried on by one's own muscles. The charm, however, is that even a walk in London often vaguely recalls better places and nobler forms of the exercise. Wordsworth's Susan hears a thrush at the corner of Wood Street, and straightway sees

> "A mountain ascending, a vision of trees,
> Bright volumes of vapour through Lothbury glide,
> And a river flows on through the vale of Cheapside."

The gulls which seem lately to have found out the merits of London give to occasional Susans, I hope, a whiff of fresh sea-breezes. But, even without gulls or wood-pigeons, I can often find occasions in the heart of London for recalling the old memories, without any definable pretext; little pictures of scenery, sometimes assignable to no definable place, start up invested with a faint aroma of old friendly walks and solitary meditations and strenuous exercise, and I feel convinced that, if I am not a thorough scoundrel, I owe that relative excellence to the harmless monomania which so often took me, to appropriate Bunyan's phrase, from the amusements of *Vanity Fair* to the *Delectable Mountains* of pedestrianism.

Leslie Stephen.

The Exhilarations of the Road

Afoot and light-hearted I take to the open road.
                                    WHITMAN.

Occasionally on the sidewalk, amid the dapper, swiftly-moving, high-heeled boots and gaiters, I catch a glimpse of the naked human foot. Nimbly it scuffs along, the toes spread, the sides flatten, the heel protrudes; it grasps the curbing, or bends to the form of the uneven surfaces,—a thing sensuous and alive, that seems to take cognisance of whatever it touches or passes. How primitive and uncivil it looks in such company,—a real barbarian in the parlour. We are so unused to the human anatomy, to simple, unadorned nature, that it looks a little repulsive; but it is beautiful for all that. Though it be a black foot and an unwashed foot, it shall be exalted. It is a thing of life amid leather, a free spirit amid cramped, a wild bird amid caged, an athlete amid consumptives. It is the symbol of my order, the Order of Walkers. That unhampered, vitally playing piece of anatomy is the type of the pedestrian, man returned to first principles, in direct contact and intercourse with the earth and the elements, his faculties unsheathed, his mind plastic, his body toughened, his heart light, his soul dilated: while those cramped and distorted members in the calf and kid are the unfortunate wretches doomed to carriages and cushions.

I am not going to advocate the disuse of boots and shoes, or the abandoning of the improved modes of travel; but I am going to brag as lustily as I can on behalf of the pedestrian, and show how all the shining angels second and accompany the man who goes afoot, while all the dark spirits are ever looking out for a chance to ride.

When I see the discomforts that able-bodied American men will put up with rather than go a mile or half a mile on foot, the abuses they will tolerate and encourage, crowding the street car on a little fall in the temperature or the appearance of an inch or two of snow, packing up to overflowing, dangling to the straps, treading on each other's toes, breathing each other's breaths, crushing the women and children, hanging by tooth and nail to a square inch of the platform, imperilling their limbs and killing the horses,—I think the commonest tramp in the street has good reason to felicitate himself on his rare privilege of going afoot. Indeed, a race that neglects or despises this primitive gift, that fears the touch of the soil, that has no footpaths, no community of ownership in the land which they imply, that warns off the walker as a trespasser, that knows no way but the highway, the carriage-way, that forgets the stile, the footbridge, that even ignores the rights of the pedestrian in the public road, providing no escape for him but in the ditch or up the bank, is in a fair way to far more serious degeneracy.

Shakespeare makes the chief qualification of the walker a merry heart:—

> "Jog on, jog on the footpath way,
> And merrily hent the stile-a;
> A merry heart goes all the day,
> Your sad tires in a mile-a."

The human body is a steed that goes freest and longest under a light rider, and the lightest of all riders is a cheerful heart. Your sad, or morose, or embittered, or preoccupied heart settles heavily into the saddle, and the poor beast, the body, breaks down the first mile. Indeed, the heaviest thing in the world is a heavy heart. Next to that the most burdensome to the walker is a heart not in perfect sympathy and accord with the body—a reluctant or unwilling heart. The horse and rider must not only both be willing to go the same way, but the rider must lead the way and infuse his own lightness and eagerness into the steed. Herein is no doubt our trouble and one reason of the decay of the noble art in this country. We are unwilling walkers. We are not innocent and simple-hearted enough to enjoy a walk. We have fallen from that state of grace which capacity to enjoy a walk implies. It cannot be said that as a people we are so positively sad, or morose, or melancholic as that we are vacant of that sportiveness and surplusage of animal spirits that characterised our ancestors, and that springs from full and harmonious life,—a sound heart in accord with a sound body. A man must invest himself near at hand and in common things, and be content with a steady and moderate return, if he would know the blessedness of a cheerful heart and the sweetness of a walk over the round earth. This is a lesson the American has yet to learn— capability of amusement on a low key. He expects rapid and extraordinary returns. He would make the very elemental laws pay usury. He has nothing to invest in a walk; it is too slow, too cheap. We crave the astonishing, the exciting, the far away, and do not know the highways of the gods when we see them,—always a sign of the decay of the faith and simplicity of man.

If I say to my neighbour, "Come with me, I have great wonders to show you," he pricks up his ears and comes forthwith; but when I take him on the hills under the full blaze of the sun, or along the country road, our footsteps lighted by the moon and stars, and say to him, "Behold, these are the wonders, these are the circuits of the gods, this we now tread is a morning star," he feels defrauded, and as if I had played him a trick. And yet nothing less than dilatation and enthusiasm like this is the badge of the master walker.

If we are not sad we are careworn, hurried, discontented, mortgaging the present for the promise of the future. If we take a walk, it is as we take a prescription, with about the same relish and with about the same purpose; and the more the fatigue the greater our faith in the virtue of the medicine.

Of those gleesome saunters over the hills in spring, or those sallies of the body in winter, those excursions into space when the foot strikes fire at every step, when the air tastes like a new and finer mixture, when we accumulate force and gladness as we go along, when the sight of objects by the roadside and of the fields and woods pleases more than pictures or than all the art in the world,—those ten or twelve mile dashes that are but the wit and affluence of the corporeal powers,—of such diversion and open road entertainment, I say, most of us know very little.

I notice with astonishment that at our fashionable watering-places nobody walks; that of all those vast crowds of health-seekers and lovers of country air, you can never catch one in the fields or woods, or guilty of trudging along the country road with dust on his shoes and sun-tan on his hands and face. The sole amusement seems to be to eat and dress and sit about the hotels and glare at each other. The men look bored, the women look tired, and all seem to sigh, "O Lord! what shall we do to be happy and not be vulgar?" Quite different from our British cousins across the water, who have plenty of amusement and hilarity, spending most of the time at their watering-places in the open air, strolling, picnicking, boating, climbing, briskly walking, apparently with little fear of sun-tan or of compromising their "gentility."

It is indeed astonishing with what ease and hilarity the English walk. To an American it seems a kind of infatuation. When Dickens was in this country I imagine the aspirants to the honour of a walk with him were not numerous. In a pedestrian tour of England by an American, I read that "after breakfast with the Independent minister, he walked with us for six miles out of town upon our road. Three little boys and girls, the youngest six years old, also accompanied us. They were romping and rambling about all the while, and their morning walk must have been as much as fifteen miles; but they thought nothing of it, and when we parted were apparently as fresh as when they started, and very loath to return."

I fear, also, the American is becoming disqualified for the manly art of walking, by a falling off in the size of his foot. He cherishes and cultivates this part of his anatomy, and apparently thinks his taste and good breeding are to be inferred from its diminutive size. A small, trim foot, well booted or gaitered, is the national vanity. How we stare at the big feet of foreigners, and wonder what may be the price of leather in those countries, and where all the aristocratic blood is, that these plebeian extremities so predominate. If we were admitted to the confidences of the shoemaker to Her Majesty or to His Royal Highness, no doubt we would modify our views upon this latter point, for a truly large and royal nature is never stunted in the extremities; a little foot never yet supported a great character.

It is said that Englishmen when they first come to this country are for some time under the impression that American women all have deformed feet, they are so coy of them and so studiously careful to keep them hid. That there is an astonishing difference between the women of the two countries in this respect, every traveller can testify; and that there is a difference equally astonishing between the pedestrian habits and capabilities of the rival sisters is also certain.

The English pedestrian, no doubt, has the advantage of us in the matter of climate; for notwithstanding the traditional gloom and moroseness of English skies, they have in that country none of those relaxing, sinking, enervating days, of which we have so many here, and which seem especially trying to the female constitution—days which withdraw all support from the back and loins, and render walking of all things burdensome. Theirs is a climate of which it has been said that "it invites men abroad more days in the year and more hours in the day than that of any other country."

Then their land is threaded with paths which invite the walker, and which are scarcely less important than the highways. I heard of a surly nobleman near London who took it into his head to close a footpath that passed through his estate near his house, and open another one a little farther off. The pedestrians objected; the matter got into the courts, and after protracted litigation the aristocrat was beaten. The path could not be closed or moved. The memory of man ran not to the time when there was not a footpath there, and every pedestrian should have the right of way there still.

I remember the pleasure I had in the path that connects Stratford-on-Avon with Shottery, Shakespeare's path when he went courting Anne Hathaway. By the king's highway the distance is somewhat farther, so there is a well-worn path along the hedgerows and through the meadows and turnip patches. The traveller in it has the privilege of crossing the railroad track, an unusual privilege in England, and one denied to the lord in his carriage, who must either go over or under it. (It is a privilege, is it not, to be allowed the forbidden, even if it be the privilege of being run over by the engine?) In strolling over the South Downs, too, I was delighted to find that where the hill was steepest some benefactor of the order of walkers had made notches in the sward, so that the foot could bite the better and firmer; the path became a kind of stairway, which I have no doubt the ploughman respected.

When you see an English country church withdrawn, secluded, out of the reach of wheels, standing amid grassy graves and surrounded by noble trees, approached by paths and shaded lanes, you appreciate more than ever this beautiful habit of the people. Only a race that knows how to use its feet, and holds footpaths sacred, could put such a charm of privacy and humility into such a structure. I think I should be tempted to go to church myself if I saw all my neighbours starting off across the fields or along paths that led to such charmed spots, and was sure I would not be jostled or run over by the rival chariots of the worshippers at the temple doors. I think this is what ails our religion; humility and devoutness of heart leave one when he lays by his walking shoes and walking clothes, and sets out for church drawn by something.

Indeed, I think it would be tantamount to an astonishing revival of religion if the people would all walk to church on Sunday and walk home again. Think how the stones would preach to them by the wayside; how their benumbed minds would warm up beneath the friction of the gravel; how their vain and foolish thoughts, their desponding thoughts, their besetting demons of one kind and another, would drop behind them, unable to keep up or to endure the fresh air. They would walk away from their *ennui*, their worldly cares, their uncharitableness, their pride of dress; for these devils always want to ride, while the simple virtues are never so happy as when on foot. Let us walk by all means; but if we will ride, get an ass.

Then the English claim that they are a more hearty and robust people than we are. It is certain they are a plainer people, have plainer tastes, dress plainer, build plainer, speak plainer, keep closer to facts, wear broader shoes and coarser clothes, place a lower estimate on themselves, etc.—all of which traits favour pedestrian habits. The English grandee is not confined to his carriage; but if the American aristocrat leaves his, he is ruined. Oh, the weariness, the emptiness, the plotting, the seeking rest and finding none, that goes by in the carriages! while your pedestrian is always cheerful, alert, refreshed, with his heart in his hand and his hand free to all. He looks down upon nobody; he is on the common level. His pores are all open, his circulation is active, his digestion good. His heart is not cold, nor his faculties asleep. He is the only real traveller; he alone tastes the "gay, fresh sentiment of the road." He is not isolated, but one with things, with the farms and industries on either hand. The vital, universal currents play through him. He knows the ground is alive; he feels the pulses of the wind, and reads the mute language of things. His sympathies are all aroused; his senses are continually reporting messages to his mind. Wind, frost, rain, heat, cold, are something to him. He is not merely a spectator of the panorama of nature, but a participator in it. He experiences the country he passes through—tastes it, feels it, absorbs it; the traveller in his fine carriage sees it merely. This gives the fresh charm to that class of books that may be called "Views Afoot," and to the narratives of hunters, naturalists, exploring parties, etc. The walker does not need a large territory. When you get into a railway car you want a continent, the man in his carriage requires a township; but a walker like Thoreau finds as much and more along the shores of Walden Pond. The former, as it were, has merely time to glance at the headings of the chapters, while the latter need not miss a line, and Thoreau reads between the lines. Then the walker has the privilege of the fields, the woods, the hills, the by-ways. The apples by the roadside are for him, and the berries, and the spring of water, and the friendly shelter; and if the weather is cold, he eats the frost grapes and the persimmons, or even the white meated turnip, snatched from the field he passed through, with incredible relish.

Afoot and in the open road, one has a fair start in life at last. There is no hindrance now. Let him put his best foot forward. He is on the broadest humane plane. This is on the level of all the great laws and heroic deeds. From this platform he is eligible to any good fortune. He was sighing for the golden age; let him walk to it. Every step brings him nearer. The youth of the world is but a few days' journey distant. Indeed, I know persons who think they have walked back to that fresh aforetime of a single bright Sunday in autumn or early spring. Before noon they felt its airs upon their cheeks, and by nightfall, on the banks of some quiet stream, or along some path in the wood, or on some hill-top, aver they have heard the voices and felt the wonder and the mystery that so enchanted the early races of men.

I think if I could walk through a country I should not only see many things and have adventures that I should otherwise miss, but that I should come into relations with that country at first hand, and with the men and women in it, in a way that would afford the deepest satisfaction. Hence I envy the good fortune of all walkers, and feel like joining myself to every tramp that comes along. I am jealous of the clergyman I read about the other day who footed it from Edinburgh to London, as poor Effie Deans did, carrying her shoes in her hand most of the way, and over the ground that rugged Ben Jonson strode, larking it to Scotland, so long ago. I read with longing of the pedestrian feats of college youths, so gay and light-hearted, with their coarse shoes on their feet and their knapsacks on their backs. It would have been a good draught of the rugged cup to have walked with Wilson the ornithologist, deserted by his companions, from Niagara to Philadelphia through the snows of winter. I almost wish that I had been born to the career of a German mechanic, that I might have had that delicious adventurous year of wandering over my country before I settled down to work. I think how much richer and firmer-grained life would be to me if I could journey afoot through Florida and Texas, or follow the windings of the Platte or the Yellowstone, or stroll through Oregon, or browse for a season about Canada. In the bright inspiring days of autumn I only want the time and the companion to walk back to the natal spot, the family nest, across two States and into the mountains of a third. What adventures we would have by the way, what hard pulls, what prospects from hills, what spectacles we would behold of night and day, what passages with dogs, what glances, what peeps into windows, what characters we should fall in with, and how seasoned and hardy we should arrive at our destination!

For companion I should want a veteran of the war! Those marches put something into him I like. Even at this distance his mettle is but little softened. As soon as he gets warmed up it all comes back to him. He catches your step and away you go, a gay, adventurous, half predatory couple. How quickly he falls into the old ways of jest and anecdote and song! You may have known him for years without having heard him hum an air, or more than casually revert to the subject of his experience during the war. You have even questioned and cross-questioned him without firing the train you wished. But get him out on a vacation tramp, and you can walk it all out of him. By the camp-fire at night or swinging along the streams by day, song, anecdote, adventure, come to the surface, and you wonder how your companion has kept silent so long.

It is another proof of how walking brings out the true character of a man. The devil never yet asked his victims to take a walk with him. You will not be long in finding your companion out. All disguises will fall away from him. As his pores open his character is laid bare. His deepest and most private self will come to the top. It matters little whom you ride with, so he be not a pickpocket; for both of you will, very likely, settle down closer and firmer in your reserve, shaken down like a measure of corn by the jolting as the journey proceeds. But walking is a more vital copartnership; the relation is a closer and more sympathetic one, and you do not feel like walking ten paces with a stranger without speaking to him.

Hence the fastidiousness of the professional walker in choosing or admitting a companion, and hence the truth of a remark of Emerson that you will generally fare better to take your dog than to invite your neighbour. Your cur-dog is a true pedestrian, and your neighbour is very likely a small politician. The dog enters thoroughly into the spirit of the enterprise; he is not indifferent or preoccupied; he is constantly sniffing adventure, laps at every spring, looks upon every field and wood as a new world to be explored, is ever on some fresh trail, knows something important will happen a little farther on, gazes with the true wonder-seeing eyes, whatever the spot or whatever the road finds it good to be there—in short, is just that happy, delicious, excursive vagabond that touches one at so many points, and whose human prototype in a companion robs miles and leagues of half their power to fatigue.

Persons who find themselves spent in a short walk to the market or the post-office, or to do a little shopping, wonder how it is that their pedestrian friends can compass so many weary miles and not fall down from sheer exhaustion; ignorant of the fact that the walker is a kind of projectile that drops far or near according to the expansive force of the motive that set it in motion, and that it is easy enough to regulate the charge according to the distance to be traversed. If I am loaded to carry only one mile and am compelled to walk three, I generally feel more fatigue than if I had walked six under the proper impetus of pre-adjusted resolution. In other words, the will or corporeal mainspring, whatever it be, is capable of being wound up to different degrees of tension, so that one may walk all day nearly as easy as half that time if he is prepared beforehand. He knows his task, and he measures and distributes his powers accordingly. It is for this reason that an unknown road is always a long road. We cannot cast the mental eye along it and see the end from the beginning. We are fighting in the dark, and cannot take the measure of our foe. Every step must be preordained and provided for in the mind. Hence also the fact that to vanquish one mile in the woods seems equal to compassing three in the open country. The furlongs are ambushed, and we magnify them.

Then, again, how annoying to be told it is only five miles to the next place when it is really eight or ten! We fall short nearly half the distance, and are compelled to urge and roll the spent ball the rest of the way.

In such a case walking degenerates from a fine art to a mechanic art; we walk merely; to get over the ground becomes the one serious and engrossing thought; whereas success in walking is not to let your right foot know what your left foot doeth. Your heart must furnish such music that in keeping time to it your feet will carry you around the globe without knowing it. The walker I would describe takes no note of distance; his walk is a sally, a *bon mot*, an unspoken *jeu d'esprit*; the ground is his butt, his provocation; it furnishes him the resistance his body craves; he rebounds upon it, he glances off and returns again, and uses it gaily as his tool.

I do not think I exaggerate the importance or the charms of pedestrianism, or our need as a people to cultivate the art. I think it would tend to soften the national manners, to teach us the meaning of leisure, to acquaint us with the charms of the open air, to strengthen and foster the tie between the race and the land. No one else looks out upon the world so kindly and charitably as the pedestrian; no one else gives and takes so much from the country he passes through. Next to the labourer in the fields, the walker holds the closest relation to 239 the soil; and he holds a closer and more vital relation to Nature because he is freer and his mind more at leisure.

Man takes root at his feet, and at best he is no more than a potted plant in his house or carriage till he has established communication with the soil by the loving and magnetic touch of his soles to it. Then the tie of association is born; then spring those invisible fibres and rootlets through which character comes to smack of the soil, and which make a man kindred to the spot of earth he inhabits.

The roads and paths you have walked along in summer and winter weather, the fields and hills which you have looked upon in lightness and gladness of heart, where fresh thoughts have come into your mind, or some noble prospect has opened before you, and especially the quiet ways where you have walked in sweet converse with your friend, pausing under the trees, drinking at the spring—henceforth they are not the same; a new charm is added; those thoughts spring there perennial, your friend walks there for ever.

We have produced some good walkers and saunterers, and some noted climbers; but as a staple recreation, as a daily practice, the mass of the people dislike and despise walking. Thoreau said he was a good horse, but a poor roadster. I chant the virtues of the roadster as well. I sing of the sweetness of gravel, good sharp quartz-grit. It is the proper condiment for the sterner seasons, and many a human gizzard would be cured of half its ills by a suitable daily allowance of it. I think Thoreau himself would have profited immensely by it. His diet was too exclusively vegetable. A man cannot live on grass alone. If one has been a lotus-eater all summer, he must turn gravel-eater in the fall and winter. Those who have tried it know that gravel possesses an equal though an opposite charm. It spurs to action. The foot tastes it and henceforth rests not. The joy of moving and surmounting, of attrition and progression, the thirst for space, for miles and leagues of distance, for sights and prospects, to cross mountains and thread rivers, and defy frost, heat, snow, danger, difficulties, seizes it; and from that day forth its possessor is enrolled in the noble army of walkers.

John Burroughs.

www.ingramcontent.com/pod-product-compliance
Lightning Source LLC
Chambersburg PA
CBHW011255040426
42453CB00015B/2420